Mammals *of* Arizona

Field Guide

by Stan Tekiela

Adventure Publications, Inc.
Cambridge, Minnesota

To my wife, Katherine, and
daughter, Abigail, with all my love

ACKNOWLEDGMENTS

A heartfelt thanks to Rick and Nora Bowers, who greatly helped me obtain many of the photos for this book and who also carefully reviewed the range maps. Many thanks to the wonderful people whose expertise and knowledge greatly contributed to this book: Linda Kennedy, Ph.D., and Christine Hass, Ph.D., of Audubon's Appleton-Whittell Research Ranch; Karen Krebbs, Conservation Biologist; and the Arizona-Sonora Desert Museum. Special thanks to the National Wildlife Refuge System and the many public and private state and local agencies for stewarding the lands that are critical to the wild mammals we love so much.

Edited by Sandy Livoti

Cover and book design by Jonathan Norberg

Silhouettes, tracks and range maps by Anthony Hertzel

Cover photo: Bobcat by Stan Tekiela
See pages 374-375 for photo credits by photographer and page number.

10 9 8 7 6 5 4 3 2 1

Copyright 2008 by Stan Tekiela
Published by Adventure Publications, Inc.
820 Cleveland St. S
Cambridge, MN 55008
1-800-678-7006
www.adventurepublications.net
All rights reserved
Printed in China
ISBN-13: 978-1-59193-075-4
ISBN-10: 1-59193-075-8

TABLE OF CONTENTS

Introduction

The Mammals

Mice & Rats

Muskrat

Squirrels

ARIZONA'S MAMMALS

Arizona is a great place for wildlife watchers! This state is one of the few places to see magnificent mammals such as Desert Bighorn Sheep. We also have a large population of Elk, along with many interesting animals such as the Ringtail and the Abert's Squirrel. While Bobcats and Mountain Lions make their homes in the coniferous mountain forests of Arizona, the foothills are great places to catch glimpses of Mule Deer and Mountain Cottontails. In lower elevations there are jackrabbits and prairie dogs, which are always fun to watch. No matter where you may be in Arizona, there is a wide variety of mammals to see and enjoy.

Mammals of Arizona Field Guide is an easy-to-use field guide to help the curious nature lover identify all species of mammals found in Arizona. It is an all-photographic guide just for Arizona, featuring full-color images of animals in their habitats. It is one in a series of unique field guides for Arizona that includes birds, mammals, trees, wildflowers and cacti.

WHAT IS A MAMMAL?

The first mammals appeared in the late Triassic Period, about 200 million years ago. These ancient mammals were small, lacked diversity and looked nothing like our current-day mammals. During the following Jurassic Period, mammal size and diversity started to increase. Mammals generally started to appear more like today's mammals in the Cenozoic Era, which occurred after the mass extinction of dinosaurs, about 60 million years ago.

Today, modern mammals are a large group of animals that includes nearly 4,500 species around the world, with more than 400 species in North America. Here in Arizona, we have 144 species. Except for the House Mouse, Norway Rat, Black Rat, Burro and Feral Horse, the mammals of Arizona are native to the state. They range from the tiny Desert Shrew, which is no larger than a human thumb, to the extremely large and majestic Elk, which can grow to a length of nearly 10 feet (3 m) and weigh up to 1,100 pounds (495 kg).

All mammals have some common traits or characteristics. Mammals have a backbone (vertebra) and are warm-blooded (endothermic). In endothermic animals, the process of eating and breaking down food in the digestive tract produces heat, which keeps the animal warm even on cold winter nights. Except during periods of hibernation or torpor, the body temperature of mammals stays within a narrow range, just as it does in people. Body temperature is controlled with rapid, open-mouthed breathing known as panting, by shunting blood flow to or away from areas with networks of blood vessels, such as ears, for cooling or conserving heat. When blood flows through vessels that are close to the surface of skin, heat is released and the body cools. When blood flows away from the surface of skin, heat is conserved.

Most mammals are covered with a thick coat of fur or hair. Fur is critical for survival and needs to be kept clean and in good condition. In some animals, such as the Northern River Otter, the fur is so thick it keeps the underlying skin warm and dry even while swimming. Just as birds must preen their feathers to maintain good health, animals spend hours each day licking and "combing" or grooming their fur. You can easily observe this grooming behavior in your pet cat or dog.

Mammals share several other characteristics. All females bear live young and suckle their babies with milk produced from the mammary glands. Mother's milk provides young mammals with total nourishment during the first part of their lives. Also, mammals have sound-conducting bones in their middle ears. These bones give animals the ability to hear as people do and, in many cases, hear much better.

Mammals are diphyodont, meaning they have two sets of teeth. There are milk or deciduous teeth, which fall out, and permanent teeth, also known as adult teeth. Adult teeth usually consist of incisors, canines, premolars and molars, but these categories can be highly variable in each mammal family. Teeth are often used to classify or group mammals into families in the same manner as the bill of a bird is used to classify or group birds into families.

Reproduction in mammals can be complex and difficult to understand. Many mammals have delayed implantation, which means after the egg and sperm have joined (impregnation), the resulting embryo remains in a suspended state until becoming implanted in the uterine wall. The delay time can be anywhere from a few days to weeks or months. An animal that becomes stressed from lack of food will pass the embryo out of the reproductive tract, and no pregnancy occurs. Conversely, well-fed mothers may have twins or even triplets. Bats and some other species store sperm in the reproductive tract over winter. Impregnation is delayed until spring, and implantation occurs right after impregnation. This process is known as delayed impregnation.

Most mammals are nocturnal, secretive and don't make a lot of noise, so they tend to go unnoticed. Signs of mammals, such as tracks or scat, are often more commonly seen than the actual animal. However, if you spend some time in the right habitat at the right time of day, your chances of seeing mammals will increase.

IDENTIFICATION STEP-BY-STEP

Fortunately, most large mammals are easy to identify and are not confused with other species. This is not the case, however, with small mammals such as mice or voles. Small animals, while plentiful, can be a challenge to correctly identify because they often have only minor differences in teeth or internal organs and bones.

This field guide is organized by families, starting with small animals, such as shrews and mice, and ending with large mammals such as bear and horse. Within each family section, the animals are in size order from small to large.

Each mammal has four to eight pages of color photos and text, with a silhouette of the animal illustrated on the first description page. Each silhouette is located in a quick-compare tab in the upper right corner. Decide which animal group you are seeing, use the quick-compare tabs to locate the pages for that group, then compare the photos with your animal. If you aren't sure of the identity, the text on description pages explains identifying features that may or may not be easily seen. The first description page for each species also has a compare section with notes about similar species in this field guide. Other pertinent details and the naturalist facts in Stan's Notes will help you correctly identify your mammal in question. Photos of other species will help you identify all of the mammals of Arizona.

Thus, every effort has been made to provide relevant identification information including range maps, which can help you eliminate some choices. Colored areas of the maps show where a species can be seen, but not the density of the species. While ranges are accurately depicted, they change on an ongoing basis due to a variety of factors. Please use the maps as intended–as a general guide only.

Finally, if you already know the name of your animal, simply use the index to quickly find the page and learn more about the species from the text and photos.

For many people, an animal's track or silhouette is all they might see of an animal. However, tracks in mud or sand and silhouettes are frequently difficult to identify. Special quick-compare pages, beginning on page 14, are a great place to start the identification process. These pages group similar kinds of animals and tracks side by side for easy comparison. For example, all hoofed animals, such as sheep and bison, are grouped in one section and all dog-like animals are grouped in another. Within the groupings, silhouettes and tracks are illustrated in relative size from small to large. This format allows you to compare one silhouette or track shape and size with another that is similarly shaped and sized. When you don't know whether you're seeing the silhouette or track of a coyote or wolf, a deer or elk or other similar species, use the quick-compare pages for quick and easy reference.

To begin, find the group that your unknown silhouette or track looks similar to and start comparing. Since each group has relatively few animals, it won't take long to narrow your choices. A ruler can be handy to measure your track and compare it with the size given in the book. To confirm the identity of the silhouette or track and for more detailed information about the animal, refer to the description pages for the number of toes, length of stride and other distinguishing characteristics.

TAXONOMY OF ARIZONA'S MAMMALS

Biologists classify mammals based on their ancestry and physical characteristics. Arizona's mammals are grouped into eight scientific orders. Charts with the scientific classification (taxonomy) are shown on the Appendix, pages 356-367. Each of the eight charts starts with one of the orders and shows all of the scientific families and mammals in that particular order.

CAUTION

Hunting, trapping, possessing and other activities involving animals are regulated by the Arizona Game and Fish Department. You should familiarize yourself with the laws and seasons before doing any kill trapping, live trapping and hunting.

As interesting as all of these animals are, resist any temptation to capture any animal for a pet. Wild animals, even babies, never make good pets. Wild animals often have specific dietary and habitat requirements that rarely can be duplicated in a captive situation, and many will not survive. In many cases, capturing animals for pets is also illegal. This practice not only diminishes the population, it reduces the possibility for future reproduction. Furthermore, some animals are uncommon in Arizona, and their populations can be even more quickly depleted.

Live trapping of animals in an attempt to rid your yard of them rarely works. The removal of an animal from its habitat creates a void that is quickly filled with a neighboring animal or its offspring, recreating the original situation. Moreover, an unfortunate animal that is live trapped and moved to a new location often cannot find a habitat with an adequate food supply, shelter or a territory that is not already occupied. Animals that have been moved often die from exposure to weather, are struck by vehicles while crossing roads or killed by resident animals. With habitat ranges growing smaller every year, removing just one animal can have a direct impact on the local population of a species. We can all learn to live with our wild animals with just a few modifications to our yards and attitudes. Observe and record animals with your camera, but leave them where they belong–in the wild.

Encounters with wildlife often involve injured or orphaned animals. Many well-intentioned people with little or no resources or knowledge of what is needed try to care for such animals. Injured or orphaned animals deserve the best care, so please do the right thing if you find one and turn it over to a licensed professional wildlife rehabilitator. Information about wildlife rehabilitation in Arizona is listed in the resource section of this field guide. The rehabilitation staff may often be able to give you updates on the condition of an animal you bring in and even when it is released. When you take an animal to a rehab center, you might also want to consider making a monetary donation to help cover the costs involved for its care.

Enjoy the Wild Mammals!

Stan

Body length measurements
do not include tail.

Average size of the smallest and
largest of this group compared to
an 8" hand.

Silhouettes are in proportion by
average body length. Tracks are in
proportion by average largest
foot. Front track is on the left and
hind is on the right.

 2¼"

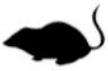

Desert Shrew
pg. 39

¼"   ⅜"

 2¼"

Northern Pygmy Mouse
pg. 64

½"   ⅞"

 3"

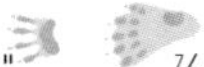

Western Jumping
Mouse pg. 51

½"   1¾"

 3⅛"

Apache Pocket Mouse
pg. 48

½"   ⅞"

 3⅜"

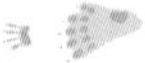

Cockrum's Gray Shrew
pg. 43

¼"   ½"

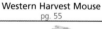 3½"

Western Harvest Mouse
pg. 55

¼"   ⅝"

 3½"

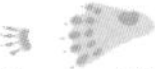

Southern Red-backed
Vole pg. 95

½"   ¾"

 3¾"

Deer Mouse
pg. 61

¼"   ¾"

 3¾"

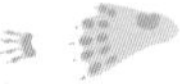

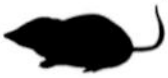

Merriam's Shrew
pg. 43

⅜"   ½"

 3¾"

Mesquite Mouse
pg. 65

½"   ¾"

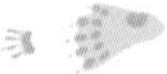

2⅜"
Arizona Pocket Mouse
pg. 48

½" ⅞"

2¾"
Little Pocket Mouse
pg. 48

½" ⅝"

2⅞"
Rock Pocket Mouse
pg. 45

½" ⅞"

3¼"
House Mouse
pg. 64

¼" ½"

3⅜"
Dwarf Shrew
pg. 43

¼" ⅜"

3⅜"
Arizona Shrew
pg. 43

¼" ½"

3½"
Desert Pocket Mouse
pg. 48

¾" 1"

3⅝"
White-footed
Mouse pg. 64

¼" ¾"

3⅝"
Long-tailed Pocket
Mouse pg. 49

½" 1"

3¾"
Southern Grasshopper
Mouse pg. 67

½" ⅞"

3¾"
Mearn's Grasshopper
Mouse pg. 71

½" ⅞"

3¾"
Cactus Mouse
pg. 64

½" 1"

Similar species on next page 15

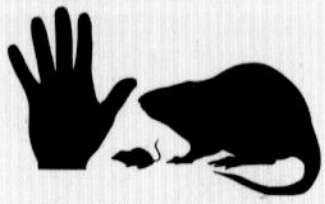

Body length measurements do not include tail.

Average size of the smallest and largest of this group compared to an 8" hand.

Silhouettes are in proportion by average body length. Tracks are in proportion by average largest foot. Front track is on the left and hind is on the right.

3¾"

Pinyon Mouse
pg. 65

¾"　1"

3¾"

Bailey's Pocket Mouse
pg. 49

⅞"　1"

4¼"

Montane Shrew
pg. 43

⅜"　½"

4¼"

Plains Harvest Mouse
pg. 59

½"　¾"

4⅝"

Hispid Pocket Mouse
pg. 49

⅞"　1⅛"

4¾"

Silky Pocket Mouse
pg. 49

½"　¾"

4¾"

Merriam's Kangaroo Rat
pg. 77

1"　1¾"

4⅞"

Long-tailed Vole
pg. 99

¾"　1⅛"

4⅞"

**Chisel-toothed
Kangaroo Rat** pg. 77

1"　1⅚"

5½"

Desert Kangaroo Rat
pg. 77

1¼"　1⅞"

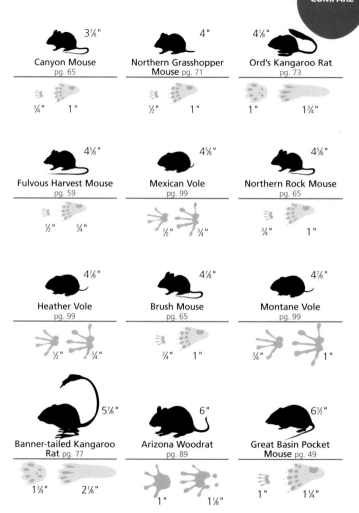

3⅞"
Canyon Mouse
pg. 65
¾"   1"

4"
Northern Grasshopper Mouse pg. 71
½"   1"

4⅛"
Ord's Kangaroo Rat
pg. 73
1"   1¾"

4⅝"
Fulvous Harvest Mouse
pg. 59
½"   ¾"

4⅝"
Mexican Vole
pg. 99
½"   ¾"

4⅝"
Northern Rock Mouse
pg. 65
¾"   1"

4⅞"
Heather Vole
pg. 99
½"   ¾"

4⅞"
Brush Mouse
pg. 65
¾"   1"

4⅞"
Montane Vole
pg. 99
¾"   1"

5⅞"
Banner-tailed Kangaroo Rat pg. 77
1¾"   2⅛"

6"
Arizona Woodrat
pg. 89
1"   1⅛"

6½"
Great Basin Pocket Mouse pg. 49
1"   1¼"

Similar species on next page   17

Body length measurements
do not include tail.

Average size of the smallest and
largest of this group compared to
an 8" hand.

Silhouettes are in proportion by
average body length. Tracks are in
proportion by average largest
foot. Front track is on the left and
hind is on the right.

6⅝"

Desert Woodrat
pg. 89

6¾"

**Yellow-nosed
Cotton Rat** pg. 83

⅞"   1⅜"

¾"   1"

7¼"

Hispid Cotton Rat
pg. 83

8⅜"

**White-throated
Woodrat** pg. 85

1"   1½"

1"   1⅜"

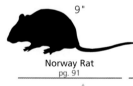

9"

Norway Rat
pg. 91

10"

Muskrat
pg. 101

1"   1½"

1½"   3"

6¾"

Tawny-bellied
Cotton Rat pg. 83

¾"   1"

6⅞"

Black Rat
pg. 93

1"   1⅜"

7¼"

Arizona Cotton Rat
pg. 79

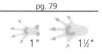

1"   1½"

8⅝"

Stephen's Woodrat
pg. 89

1"   1⅜"

8⅞"

Bushy-tailed Woodrat
pg. 89

1"   1⅛"

9"

Mexican Woodrat
pg. 89

1"   1½"

19

Body length measurements
do not include tail.

Average size of the smallest and
largest of this group compared to
an 8" hand.

Silhouettes are in proportion to
each other by average body
length.

 2¼"

**California Leaf-nosed
Bat** pg. 112

no tracks

 2¼"

**Western Small-footed
Bat** pg. 112

no tracks

2½"

Big Brown Bat
pg. 109

no tracks

2½"

Silver-haired Bat
pg. 112

no tracks

 2¾"

Yuma Myotis
pg. 113

no tracks

 2⅞"

Arizona Myotis
pg. 113

no tracks

2⅞"

Southwestern Myotis
pg. 113

no tracks

 3⅛"

Pocketed Free-tailed Bat
pg. 113

no tracks

 3⅛"

Lesser Long-nosed Bat
pg. 113

no tracks

 3¼"

**Mexican Long-tongued
Bat** pg. 113

no tracks

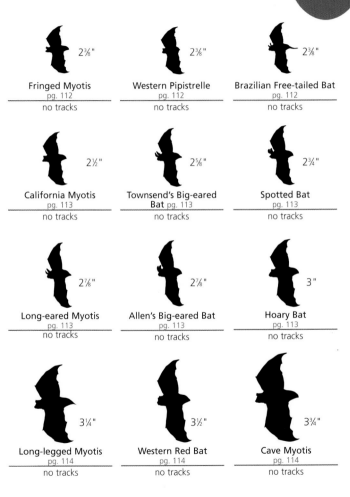

2⅜"

Fringed Myotis
pg. 112
no tracks

2⅜"

Western Pipistrelle
pg. 112
no tracks

2⅜"

Brazilian Free-tailed Bat
pg. 112
no tracks

2½"

California Myotis
pg. 113
no tracks

2⅝"

Townsend's Big-eared Bat pg. 113
no tracks

2¾"

Spotted Bat
pg. 113
no tracks

2⅞"

Long-eared Myotis
pg. 113
no tracks

2⅞"

Allen's Big-eared Bat
pg. 113
no tracks

3"

Hoary Bat
pg. 113
no tracks

3¼"

Long-legged Myotis
pg. 114
no tracks

3½"

Western Red Bat
pg. 114
no tracks

3¾"

Cave Myotis
pg. 114
no tracks

Similar species on next page 21

Body length measurements
do not include tail.

Average size of the smallest and
largest of this group compared to
an 8" hand.

Silhouettes are in proportion to
each other by average body
length.

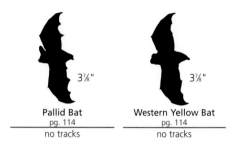

3⅞"

Pallid Bat
pg. 114

no tracks

3⅞"

Western Yellow Bat
pg. 114

no tracks

4⅞"

5⅛"

5¾"

Big Free-tailed Bat
pg. 114

no tracks

Western Mastiff Bat
pg. 114

no tracks

Underwood's Mastiff Bat pg. 114

no tracks

Body length measurements do not include tail.

Average size of the smallest and largest of this group compared to a 6' human.

Silhouettes are in proportion by average body length. Tracks are in proportion by average largest foot. Front track is on the left and hind is on the right.

3½"

Least Chipmunk
pg. 117

½" 1"

3⅝"

Hopi Chipmunk
pg. 121

⅝" 1¼"

5"

Gray-collared Chipmunk
pg. 137

⅝" 1¼"

6"

Botta's Pocket Gopher
pg. 193

⅞" ¾"

6¾"

Round-tailed Ground Squirrel pg. 153

1" 1½"

7"

Thirteen-lined Ground Squirrel pg. 157

1" 1½"

7½"

Southern Pocket Gopher
pg. 197

⅞" ¾"

10"

Abert's Squirrel
pg. 173

1½" 2⅞"

11¼"

Gunnison's Prairie Dog
pg. 185

1" 2¼"

12"

Rock Squirrel
pg. 165

1½" 2¼"

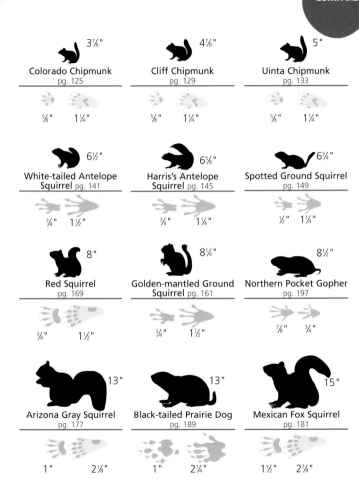

3⅞"
Colorado Chipmunk
pg. 125

⅝"   1¼"

4⅞"
Cliff Chipmunk
pg. 129

⅝"   1¼"

5"
Uinta Chipmunk
pg. 133

⅝"   1¼"

6½"
White-tailed Antelope
Squirrel pg. 141

¾"   1½"

6⅝"
Harris's Antelope
Squirrel pg. 145

¾"   1¼"

6¾"
Spotted Ground Squirrel
pg. 149

½"   1¼"

8"
Red Squirrel
pg. 169

¾"   1½"

8¼"
Golden-mantled Ground
Squirrel pg. 161

¾"   1½"

8½"
Northern Pocket Gopher
pg. 197

⅞"   ¾"

13"
Arizona Gray Squirrel
pg. 177

1"   2⅛"

13"
Black-tailed Prairie Dog
pg. 189

1"   2¼"

15"
Mexican Fox Squirrel
pg. 181

1½"   2⅞"

25

Body length measurements
do not include tail.

Average size of the smallest and
largest of this group compared to
a 6' human.

Silhouettes are in proportion by
average body length. Tracks are in
proportion by average largest
foot. Front track is on the left and
hind is on the right.

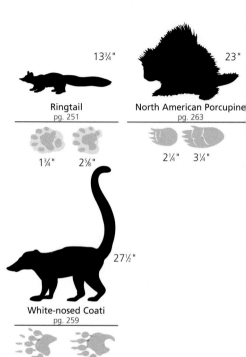

13¾"

Ringtail
pg. 251

1¾" 2⅝"

23"

North American Porcupine
pg. 263

2¼" 3¼"

27½"

White-nosed Coati
pg. 259

2¼" 3¼"

26

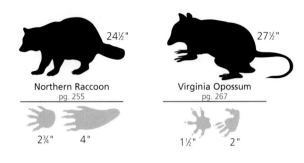

Northern Raccoon
pg. 255

24½"

2¾"   4"

Virginia Opossum
pg. 267

27½"

1½"   2"

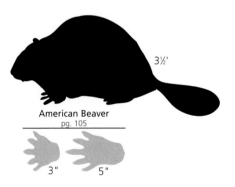

American Beaver
pg. 105

3½'

3"   5"

Body length measurements
do not include tail.

Average size of the smallest and
largest of this group compared to
a 6' human.

Mountain Cottontail
pg. 199

12 "

Desert Cottontail
pg. 203

12¾ "

1 "   3½ "   1 "   3½ "

Body length measurements
do not include tail.

Average size of the smallest and
largest of this group compared to
a 6' human.

Western Spotted Skunk
pg. 235

10¾ "

Long-tailed Weasel
pg. 219

12 "

1 "   1½ "   ¾ "   ⅞ "

Striped Skunk
pg. 247

22 "

American Badger
pg. 227

25 "

1⅜ "   2¾ "   2 "   2 "

Silhouettes are in proportion by
average body length. Tracks are in
proportion by average largest
foot. Front track is on the left and
hind is on the right.

16"

Eastern Cottontail
pg. 207

1"   3½"

21"

Black-tailed Jackrabbit
pg. 211

1"   4¾"

23½"

Antelope Jackrabbit
pg. 215

1½"   5½"

13½"

Hooded Skunk
pg. 239

1⅜" 2⅜"

15"

Hog-nosed Skunk
pg. 243

1⅜" 2¾"

17¼"

Black-footed Ferret
pg. 223

2¼" 2⅜"

36"

Northern River Otter
pg. 231

3⅜"   3½"

Body length measurements
do not include tail.

Average size of the smallest and
largest of this group compared to
a 6' human.

Kit Fox	Gray Fox
18"	23"
pg. 271	pg. 275

1½" 1⅜"   1½" 1⅜"

Body length measurements
do not include tail.

Average size of the smallest and
largest of this group compared to
a 6' human.

Ocelot	Jaguarundi
25½"	30"
pg. 291	pg. 295

2¼" 2¼"   1⅝" 1⅝"

Silhouettes are in proportion by
average body length. Tracks are in
proportion by average largest
foot. Front track is on the left and
hind is on the right.

23"

Red Fox
pg. 279

2"   1⅞"

3¼'

Coyote
pg. 283

2¼"   2⅛"

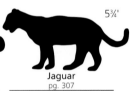
4½'

Mexican Wolf
pg. 287

5"   4⅞"

3'

Bobcat
pg. 299

2"   2"

5½'

Mountain Lion
pg. 303

5½"   5½"

5¾'

Jaguar
pg. 307

4¼"   5¾"

Body length measurements do not include tail.

Average size of the smallest and largest of this group compared to a 6' human.

Body length measurements do not include tail.

Average size of the smallest and largest of this group compared to a 6' human.

Silhouettes are in proportion by average body length. Tracks are in proportion by average largest foot. Front track is on the left and hind is on the right.

3½'

Javelina
pg. 311

1⅛ "   1 "

4¼'

Pronghorn
pg. 315

3 "   2⅞ "

5¾'

Mule Deer
pg. 323

3 "   2⅞ "

6'

Feral Horse
pg. 335

4 "   4 "

5¼'

Black Bear
pg. 347

4 "   8 "

32

4½'

4½'

5'

Burro
pg. 331

White-tailed Deer
pg. 319

Desert Bighorn Sheep
pg. 339

2½"   2½"

2¾"   2⅝"

2¾"   2⅝"

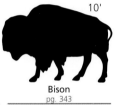

8¼'

10'

Elk
pg. 327

Bison
pg. 343

4¼"   4⅛"

6½"   6⅜"

33

Common Name

Range Map   *Scientific name*   Shape

FORMER
RANGE

Family: common family name (scientific family name)

Size: (L) average length or range of length of body from head to rump; (T) average length or range of length of tail; (H) average height or range of height to top of back

Weight: average weight or range of weight; may include (M) male and (F) female weights

Description: brief description of the mammal; may include color morphs, seasonal variations or differences between male and female

Origin/Age: native or non-native to Arizona; average life span in the wild

Compare: notes about other species that look similar and the pages on which they can be found; may include extra information to help identify

Habitat: environment (e.g., deserts, scrublands, grasslands, canyons, fields, forests); may include elevations

Home: description of nest, burrow or den; may include other related information

Food: herbivore, carnivore, insectivore, omnivore; what the animal eats most of the time; may include other related information

Sounds: vocalization or other noises the animal creates; may include variant sounds or other information

Breeding: mating season; length of gestation; may include additional comments

Young: number of offspring born per year and when; may include description or birth weight

summer coat

winter coat

silver morph   black morph

scat

Signs: evidence that the animal was there or is near; may include a description of scat; other comments

Activity: diurnal, nocturnal, crepuscular; other comments

Tracks: forepaw and hind paw or hoof size and shape, largest size first; pattern of tracks; description of prints, which may include tail drag mark or stride; other comments

Tracks and Pattern

Stan's Notes: Interesting gee-whiz natural history information. This can be something to look or listen for, or something to help positively identify the animal such as remarkable features. May include additional photos to illustrate juveniles, nests, unique behaviors and other key characteristics.

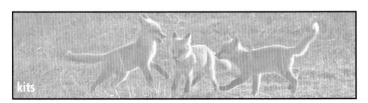

kits

Desert Shrew
Notiosorex crawfordi

Family: Shrews (Soricidae)

Size: L 2-2½" (5-6 cm); T ¾-1¼" (2-3 cm)

Weight: ⅕ oz. (6 g)

Description: Overall gray to brown with a lighter gray-to-white belly. Long pointed snout. Tiny dark eyes. Ears visible and considered large for a shrew. Tail about one-third the length of body, with a pointed tip.

Origin/Age: native; 1-2 years

Compare: The only shrew species found in the desert and Ponderosa Pine woodlands in Arizona. This is also the most common and widespread shrew in the state.

Habitat: deserts, Ponderosa Pine forests, elevations under 6,500' (1,980 m)

Home: nest made with dried plant materials, inside a woodrat pile of discarded pine cone parts (midden), under a log, brush pile or other sheltered area; does not burrow

Food: insectivore, carnivore; insects, ants, slugs, spiders, carrion

Sounds: inconsequential; sharp squeaks and high-pitched whistles

Breeding: spring to autumn mating; 18 days gestation

Young: 3-5 offspring 1-2 times per year; young are born naked with eyes closed, weaned at about 15 days, changes to a diet of regurgitated food from the mother

Signs: tiny tunnels or runways on the surface of soil; shrew is rarely, if ever, seen

Activity: nocturnal; active all year

Tracks: hind paw ⅜" (.9 cm) long, forepaw slightly smaller; 1 set of 4 tracks, but prints are so close together they appear as 1 track; 4 prints together are 1" square (6.4 sq. cm), sometimes with a slight tail drag mark; shrew tracks are not very common

Stan's Notes: A secretive, solitary animal with poor eyesight, as are all shrews. This is one of the smallest mammals in Arizona and the world and also the most widespread shrew in the state, but it is rarely seen due to its nocturnal lifestyle. Also called Gray Shrew.

Its long pointed snout is characteristic of all 30-plus species of shrews seen in North America. Gives off a strong musky odor, which makes it unattractive to large mammalian predators, but the scent does not seem to deter birds of prey such as owls and hawks. Heart rate will race to as many as 1,200 beats per minute when it is excited. Can die from fright when captured.

Has little body mass due to its small size, so it must feed nearly every hour to keep warm or starve to death. Like some other shrew species, Desert Shrew has a toxic saliva that helps it subdue prey. However, since its teeth are not designed for injecting the poison, it must be chewed into the prey. Moves constantly, darting about to find food. Often eats more than its own body weight daily in worms, slugs and beetles. Not an aggressive predator like other shrews, but will eat carrion. Does not hibernate.

A desirable animal to have around your home and yard because it eats many harmful insects and keeps populations of mice in check. Does not transmit rabies and is not harmful to people.

Similar species on next page

Shrews are small mammals that look similar to mice, but shrews have longer, more pointed snouts and well-haired, rather short tails. Fur color ranges from gray to brown or black.

All shrew species in Arizona eat insects and other small animals. With extremely high metabolic rates, they forage for food round-the-clock, consuming their body weight in food every 24 hours. Shrews are the only known mammal to have a toxic saliva.

They live in the shallow tunnels of other small mammals, such as voles, or beneath fallen logs and other debris. While all shrews have poor eyesight, they have an excellent sense of smell and the ability to hear in very high frequencies. Some are thought to be able to sense electromagnetic fields, enabling them to locate prey in complete darkness.

Dwarf Shrew 3-3¾"

Arizona Shrew 3-3¾"

Not for color identification.

Not pictured:
Cockrum's Gray Shrew 3-3¾"
Merriam's Shrew 3-4½"
Montane Shrew 4-4½"

43

Rock Pocket Mouse
Chaetodipus intermedius

Family: Kangaroo Rats and Pocket Mice (Heteromyidae)

Size: L 2¾-3" (7-7.5 cm); T 3-3½" (7.5-9 cm)

Weight: ½ oz. (14 g)

Description: Overall tan to yellowish brown or reddish brown with a wash of black hairs concentrated near the center of back and rump, giving a grizzled look. Can be nearly black. Stiff spiny hairs on rump. Often a thin, pale orange line on sides. White-to-cream chest, belly, legs and feet. Tail longer than body, bicolored, dark above, white below, with a tuft at tip. Large eyes. Small round ears, dark at tips, often with a white patch just under each ear.

Origin/Age: native; 1-3 years

Compare: Most other species of pocket mice (pp. 48-49) in the state are very similar in size and color.

Habitat: sagebrush, dry rocky habitats, unmowed grassy areas along fences (fencerows), ditches, elevations below 6,000' (1,830 m)

Home: nest made of dried plant material, in an underground burrow

Food: omnivore; seeds, vegetation, fruit, nuts, insects, earthworms

Sounds: inconsequential; scratching or scampering can be heard

Breeding: Apr-Jul mating; 20-23 days gestation

Young: 3-6 pups up to 2 times per year; born naked and deaf with eyes closed, juvenile is gray with a white belly

45

Signs: evidence of a burrow under clumps of vegetation, runways and surface tunnels radiating from the entrance of burrow; scat not seen

Activity: nocturnal; remains in the nest during the coldest winter days or during heavy rain in summer

Tracks: hind paw ⅞" (2.3 cm) long with 5 toes, forepaw ½" (1 cm) long with 4 toes; 1 set of 4 tracks along trails leading to and from the burrow

Stan's Notes: A species that can have highly variable color, often matching the color of soil in which it lives. Body size varies from region to region. Males are slightly larger than the females (sexual dimorphism) and also have a larger snout, head and jaw. Almost always associated with rocks, talus slopes and rocky deserts with sparse vegetation.

Feeds mainly on seeds (granivorous). Will gather larger seeds and transport them in its fur-lined cheek pouches, hence the common name "Pocket Mouse." Stores seeds in its underground burrow to eat later. Also eats insects when they are available (insectivorous).

Digs shallow burrows with several chambers only a few inches deep, with several entrances. Plugs the entrance holes to burrow in safety during the day.

Usually active aboveground in Arizona only from March through October. Not a true hibernator, but thought to enter a state of deep sleep known as torpor during cold spells in winter.

Home ranges are very small, with most adults spending their entire life in an area less than 20 feet (6.1 m) wide. Males have a slightly larger territory than females.

Similar species on next page

Despite the common name "Mouse," pocket mice are not a type of mouse, nor are they closely related to any other mammal species in North America. Pocket mice are found only west of the Mississippi River, where they are mainly seen in open grassy fields and deserts. They live underground in burrows and prefer sandy soil, which allows them to dig more easily into the earth.

All pocket mice are nocturnal. Unlike jumping mice, they are not good jumpers. They have coarse fur, often with stiff bristles, and fur-lined cheek pouches to carry food and nesting material–the reason for the term "Pocket" in their common names.

Arizona Pocket Mouse 2-2¾"

Little Pocket Mouse 2¼-3¾"

Apache Pocket Mouse 2¾-3½"

Desert Pocket Mouse 3¼-3¾"

Long-tailed Pocket Mouse 3¾-4"

Bailey's Pocket Mouse 3¼-4¼"

Hispid Pocket Mouse 4¼-5"

Silky Pocket Mouse 4½-5"

Great Basin Pocket Mouse 5½-7½"

Western Jumping Mouse
Zapus princeps

Family: Jumping Mice (Dipodidae)

Size: L 2½-3½" (6-9 cm); T 5-6" (13-15 cm)

Weight: ¾ oz. (21 g)

Description: A reddish brown back with lighter, sometimes yellowish sides. May have a dark stripe down the center of back. Long guard hairs give it a grizzled appearance. White belly hair. Small round ears with a thin border of white hairs. Prominent dark eyes. Long snout. Extremely long tail, dark above and white below, not tufted.

Origin/Age: native; 1-2 years

Compare: The only jumping mouse species in Arizona. Seen only in a very limited range, so use the range map to help identify. The hind feet on jumping mice are larger than other species of mice.

Habitat: along the sides of streams, willow thickets, bogs, marshes, elevations from 6,000-11,500' (1,830-3,510 m)

Home: nest made from dried grass, under a fallen log or clump of grass; used for hibernation

Food: herbivore, insectivore; underground fungi, seeds, fruit, insects

Sounds: inconsequential; scratching or scampering can be heard, drums front feet on ground if threatened

Breeding: May-Jul mating; 17-21 days gestation; will mate shortly after emerging from hibernation

Young: 4-7 pups 2 or more times per year; born naked with eyes closed

Signs: surface runways leading in many directions, grasses with missing seed heads (topped), piles of grass stems that are the same length and have seed heads removed

Activity: nocturnal; active 5-6 months of the year, hibernating from October to April or May

Tracks: hind paw 1¾" (4.5 cm) long with a long narrow heel and 5 toes, forepaw ½" (1 cm) long with 4 toes; 1 set of 4 tracks; tracks with tail drag mark seen only in mud during months of activity

Stan's Notes: The jumping mouse got its name from its ability to leap up to 3 feet (1 m) to escape predators or when it is startled. Although the name implies that it jumps to get around, it usually walks on all four feet or moves in a series of small jumps.

Often will remain motionless after jumping several times. Uses its long tail, which is more than 50 percent of its total length, for balance while jumping. Hind legs are longer than front legs and are very fragile, often breaking when live-trapped for research.

Feeds in summer on *Endogone*, an underground fungus that it finds by smell. Does not store food for winter, feeding heavily instead during the last month before it hibernates. Gains up to 100 percent of its body weight in fat. A true hibernator, inactive in winter. Male emerges from hibernation in April, female two weeks later. Some studies show that many may not survive the winter, as only half the population appears the next spring.

Matures sexually before 1 year of age. Many females born in spring are breeding in July. Adults reproduce two times or more each year.

Doesn't cause crop damage. Will rarely enter a dwelling. Jumping mice (genera *Zapus* and *Napaeozapus*) are only in North America.

Western Harvest Mouse
Reithrodontomys megalotis

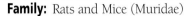

Family: Rats and Mice (Muridae)

Size: L 3-4" (7.5-10 cm); T 1-2" (2.5-5 cm)

Weight: ½-¾ oz. (14-21 g)

Description: A brown back with a wide, darker brown stripe (not readily noticeable) down the center of back. Light brown sides. White-to-gray belly. Obvious ears. Large eyes. Tail is distinctly bicolored, dark on top and light on the bottom, length equal to or longer than head and body length, not tufted.

Origin/Age: native; 1-2 years

Compare: Smaller than Fulvous Harvest Mouse (pg. 59), which has distinctive orange sides. The Plains Harvest Mouse (pg. 59) is larger and grayer than Western Harvest Mouse.

Habitat: low deserts, dry grassy areas, fields, roadsides, wet areas, marshes

Home: ball-shaped nest made of dried grass, 5-6" (13-15 cm) wide, entrance hole often at the bottom, inner chamber is lined with fine plant material, on the ground, occasionally low in a shrub or small tree or attached to grass stems

Food: herbivore, insectivore; seeds, vegetation, fruit, fresh green shoots in spring, insects

Sounds: inconsequential; high-pitched trilling call

Breeding: early spring to late autumn mating; 23-24 days gestation

Young: 1-9 (average 2-6) pups up to 4 times per year; born naked with eyes closed and weighing about ¹⁄₁₆ oz. (2 g)

Signs: surface runways, ball-shaped nest made of dried grass on the ground, most obvious after a field or grassland fire, nest is sometimes attached to grass stems or in a small tree or shrub

Activity: mostly nocturnal; active year-round, often huddles in nest during the day with other members of its family

Tracks: hind paw ⅝" (1.5 cm) long with 5 toes, forepaw ¼" (.6 cm) long with 4 toes; sometimes has a tail drag mark

Stan's Notes: This mouse is found from Illinois to California, but is more common in western states. Harvests dried grass to build its large softball-sized nest, hence the common name. Known to use the nest of a bird. Will construct its ball-shaped nest in the cup of a bird nest. May use more than one nest in its home range. Uses the runways and burrows of other animals such as pocket gophers and voles.

Considered to be a good mouse to have around because it feeds heavily on weed seeds. Stores many seeds in underground caches. A big climber, jumping into trees and shrubs and scurrying about among the branches. Non-territorial and tolerant of one another. Rarely enters homes or other buildings.

A female usually has up to four litters per season. However, it has been reported that a captive female reproduced 14 times, giving birth to a total of 58 young.

Similar species on next page 57

Harvest mice are a group of small mice that look like miniature Deer Mice (pg. 61) with long narrow tails. They are classified in a separate genus because they have a groove front-and-center in their upper incisor teeth that other small mice lack. Although some species of jumping mice and pocket mice also have grooved incisors like harvest mice, this is not a feature that the casual observer will see.

There are five species of harvest mice in the United States, three of which occur in Arizona. All harvest mouse species live in grassy areas, feed on grass seeds and build softball-sized nests of dried plant material.

The Plains Harvest Mouse occurs in the southeastern part of the state, with its range reaching into central Arizona. Its tail length is shorter than the head and body length, and its fur is overall paler than that of the Fulvous Harvest Mouse. The Fulvous occurs only in the far southeastern corner of Arizona. Its tail is at least as long as the length of its head and body, and it has coarse fur, giving a grizzled effect, with distinct orange sides.

Plains Harvest Mouse 4-4½"

Fulvous Harvest Mouse 4¼-5"

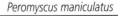

Deer Mouse
Peromyscus maniculatus

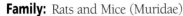

Family: Rats and Mice (Muridae)

Size: L 3-4½" (7.5-11 cm); T 2-4" (5-10 cm)

Weight: ⅜-1¼ oz. (11-35 g)

Description: Back and sides highly variable in color from gray to reddish brown. Chest, belly, legs and feet are always white. Tail sharply bicolored, dark above and white below, equal to or shorter than head and body length, with a tufted tip. Large bulging eyes. Large round ears.

Origin/Age: native; 1-2 years

Compare: The most common mouse species in the entire state. The tail of the Deer Mouse is slightly longer than that of the White-footed Mouse (pg. 64). However, it is extremely hard to differentiate these species because of their remarkable similarities.

Habitat: nearly all habitats including deserts, scrublands, woodlands, mountains, fields, wet areas, around dwellings, all elevations

Home: nest made of dried plant material and moss, in a small depression in the ground or in an above-ground cavity

Food: omnivore; seeds, vegetation, fruit, nuts, insects, earthworms, baby birds, baby mice, carrion

Sounds: inconsequential; scratching or scampering can be heard, drums front feet on ground if threatened

Breeding: Mar-Oct mating; 21-25 days gestation

Young: 1-8 (average 5) pups up to 3 times per year; born naked and deaf with eyes closed, juvenile is gray with a white belly, leaves mother at 3 weeks

Signs: strong smell of urine in the areas it often visits, including its large nest made from dried plant material; small, hard black droppings the size of a pinhead

Activity: nocturnal, crepuscular; active year-round, stays in nest during the coldest winter days or during heavy rain in summer

Tracks: hind paw ¾" (2 cm) long with 5 toes, forepaw ¼" (.6 cm) long with 4 toes; 1 set of 4 tracks; sometimes has a tail drag mark

Stan's Notes: The most common mouse in Arizona and the most widespread rodent in North America. Found in just about every habitat from the snowy Arctic Circle to the rain forests in Central America. More than 100 subspecies have been described, with the desert form occurring in Arizona; differences are in tail length and ear size. Deer Mice look different in different parts of the world (morphologically variable), more so than other mouse species.

An important food source for other animals such as foxes, hawks, coyotes and owls. Lives mostly on the ground. Tunnels beneath leaf litter to the surface of the ground and also runs around on top of the ground. May have several emergency escape tunnels in addition to the tunnel that leads to its nest.

Very tame and not aggressive. Climbs trees and shrubs to reach seeds and leaves. Caches food for winter, storing seeds and small nuts in protected areas outside the nest.

Constructs nest during late fall or early winter in a bluebird nest box or another birdhouse. Frequently solitary, but will gather in small groups in winter, usually females with young, to huddle and conserve heat. However, their combined urine quickly soaks the nesting material, necessitating a move to another nest box or natural cavity. Readily enters homes looking for shelter and food.

Sexually mature at 5-7 weeks. Male may stay with female briefly after mating, but frequently lives a solitary life. Female is more territorial than the male, but male has a larger home range. Home territory ranges from a few hundred square feet to a couple acres.

A primary host for the virulent hantavirus that causes Hantaviral Pulmonary Syndrome (HPS), a serious disease in people. Great care must be taken not to breathe in dust or other debris when cleaning out a Deer Mouse nest from a birdhouse or your home.

Similar species on next page

To many people, all mice look the same. There are many common features among species that make differentiation very difficult. To make things worse, some species hybridize, creating varieties that defy identification. While some species, such as the House Mouse, can be best identified by where they are found, firm identification of mice should be left to the experts.

Northern Pygmy Mouse 2-2½"

House Mouse 2½-4"

White-footed Mouse 3-4½"

Cactus Mouse 3-4½"

Pinyon Mouse 3½-4"

Northern Rock Mouse 4-5¼"

Brush Mouse 4¼-5½"

Not pictured:
Mesquite Mouse 3½-4"
Canyon Mouse 3½-4¼"

Southern Grasshopper Mouse
Onychomys torridus

Family: Rats and Mice (Muridae)

Size: L 3-4½" (7.5-11 cm); T 2-2¼" (5-5.5 cm)

Weight: 1 oz. (28 g)

Description: Stout, thick-bodied mouse. Brown to gray above, white below. Often has a white patch in front of ears. Short, thick bicolored tail, dark above, light below, white tipped, not well furred or tufted. Tail less than one-third the length of head and body.

Origin/Age: native; 1-3 years

Compare: Stocky-bodied mouse with a short tail. Northern Grasshopper Mouse (pg. 71) is slightly larger and occurs throughout Arizona. Mearn's Grasshopper Mouse (pg. 71) is only in southeastern Arizona. Consider the range to help identify.

Habitat: deserts (especially scrubby deserts), grasslands

Home: nest made of dried plant material, in a network of tunnels with short escape tunnels; digs tunnels or takes other animal burrows, plugs tunnels each morning to retain moisture and seal out predators

Food: omnivore; grasshoppers, other insects, spiders, plants, seeds, nuts, mice, other small mammals

Sounds: unusual high-pitched and drawn-out call, can be heard up to 50' (15 m); sharp dog-like bark when alarmed, defending territory or looking for mates, bark is like a coyote bark, but much quieter

Breeding: May-Jul mating; 26-32 days gestation

Young: 1-6 (average 3-4) pups 2-3 times per year; born naked with eyes closed, eyes open at 14 days, weaned at 3 weeks

Signs: discarded insect parts such as wings and legs, network of aboveground runways leading to and from entrances to many small escape tunnels; scat not seen because this mouse defecates in underground chambers; can sometimes be heard vocalizing

Activity: nocturnal; active year-round, most active on moonless or overcast nights, may remain in nest during the coldest parts of winter or extremely hot parts of summer

Tracks: hind paw ⅞" (2.3 cm) long with 5 toes, forepaw ½" (1 cm) long with 4 toes

Stan's Notes: Three species of grasshopper mice in Arizona, with the Southern slightly more common than Northern Grasshopper Mouse (pg. 71), although not as widespread. Found in desert habitats across half of Arizona unlike the Northern, which occurs throughout the state.

An omnivore and true insectivore. A good mouse to have around due to its consumption of grasshoppers, beetles, caterpillars and other insects. Feeds heavily on grasshoppers, hence the common name. When it senses a grasshopper nearby, it quickly grabs and bites the prey behind its head to immobilize it. Will sometimes leave the paralyzed bug for consumption later. Other times it quickly eats the head and body, leaving the legs and wings.

The genus name *Onychomys* means "clawed mouse." Claws and the unusually long toes on the front feet help it manipulate large grasshoppers and the many other insects it eats. Molar teeth have very high cusps, allowing it to chew insect exoskeletons. Enlarged muscles in its jaw increase the biting and chewing power. Able to store an entire grasshopper in its mouth to carry short distances.

Its life as a predatory mouse is very unusual and has been the subject of many studies. A very territorial animal, it scent marks posts with secretions from its anal glands. Dominant grasshopper mice will catch and kill subordinates that enter their territory.

Moves about in an extensive network of tunnels with connecting chambers. Each chamber is used for a specific activity such as food storage, defecating or nesting. Uses its short escape tunnels to retreat from threats.

Similar species on next page

Grasshopper mice are a unique group of small mice with short tails. They are more carnivorous than the other species of mice, actively hunting a wide variety of large insects and other small mammals such as other mice.

The courtship ritual of the grasshopper mouse is one of the most complex known for rodents. It involves a sequence of circling, mutual grooming and sniffing before copulation. Mated pairs will defend their food, young and homes from other mice, predators and even people. In addition to a strong bond between mates, mothers and pups have an unusually strong bond, with mothers defending their young from threats and grooming their pups before they are able to groom themselves. Fathers play a major role in raising their young, which is not the case with the other species of mice.

There are four species of grasshopper mice, but only three occur in Arizona. Northern Grasshopper Mouse is the largest of the three and has the most widespread range, occurring throughout the state. Like other grasshopper mice, it announces its territory with loud single-note whistles, given while standing on its hind legs.

The Mearn's Grasshopper Mouse appears visually identical to the Southern Grasshopper Mouse, but was recently separated into a different species when it was found to be genetically different. In Arizona, the Mearn's is found only in the far southeastern corner of the state.

Mearn's Grasshopper Mouse 3-4½"

Northern Grasshopper Mouse 3-5"

Ord's Kangaroo Rat
Dipodomys ordii

Family: Kangaroo Rats and Pocket Mice (Heteromyidae)

Size: L 4-4¼" (10-10.5 cm); T 4½-6" (11-15 cm)

Weight: 2-3 oz. (57-85 g)

Description: Unique rat with a big stocky body, long back legs and short front legs. Often stands up with front legs held against chest. Variable color, often yellow brown with a darker back and white chin, front legs and belly. Large eyes. Dark saddle mark over snout is variable. Short round ears. White spot above eyes and behind ears. Tail longer than body, sharply bicolored, darker above, large tuft at tip.

Origin/Age: native; 2-4 years

Compare: Merriam's Kangaroo Rat (pg. 77) has 4 toes on its hind feet. Banner-tailed Kangaroo Rat (pg. 77) is much larger and has a dark tail with a white tip.

Habitat: variety of habitats, sandy to rocky soils, deserts, grasslands, sagebrush, coniferous woodlands, elevations below 6,000' (1,830 m)

Home: network of tunnels, 2-3" (5-7.5 cm) wide and up to 6' (1.8 m) long, leading to inner chambers used for sleeping and feeding, often has several escape exits and dead-end tunnels for hiding

Food: herbivore, insectivore; seeds, nuts, insects

Sounds: low grunts, squeals and purrs; drums feet

Breeding: year-round mating; 25-30 days gestation; young females become sexually mature at 2 months

Young: 1-6 (average 4) offspring 2 times per year, as weather permits; born naked with eyes closed

73

Signs: burrows in sandy soils, sometimes with well-worn trails leading away; often seen on dirt roads at night within the path of vehicle headlights

Activity: nocturnal; active year-round, remains in burrow during rain or on very cold nights

Tracks: hind paw 1¾" (4.5 cm) long with a narrow heel and 5 toes, forepaw 1" (2.5 cm) long with 4 well-spread toes; often follows the same paths over and over, making individual tracks difficult to distinguish, but often has a tail drag mark

Stan's Notes: A distinctive and attractive rodent, hard to confuse with other types of rats or mice. Will hop on its hind feet (bipedal), but walks on all four legs similar to a kangaroo, hence its common name. When standing still, holds its front legs tightly against its chest and uses its long tail for balance and support. Uses its front feet to gather and hold seeds to eat or places them in its fur-lined cheek pouches for transporting back to the burrow.

Can be approached at night, but when disturbed it will leap and quickly run with a zigzag pattern back to the burrow to escape, thumping its hind feet at the burrow entrance before diving in for safety. Digs its own burrow, which has several entrances, interconnecting tunnels and many chambers for sleeping, food storage and waste. Solitary animals, with only one individual living in each burrow system. Blocks the entrances with sand and other plant material during the day to maintain temperature and humidity, and for safety.

There is an oil-secreting gland between its shoulders, which serves to distinguish individuals and sexes. To prevent from becoming oily and matted, it takes dust baths or sand baths regularly, rolling around on the ground to coat its fur with oil-absorbing dirt.

Most individuals can survive without drinking water, obtaining water directly from seed digestion. Will drink from surface water if available.

Similar species on next page

There are 17 kangaroo rat species in the United States. Five species are found in Arizona and most of the rest occur in California.

Kangaroo rats are some of the most easily identified rodents. They have silky fur, large eyes, distinctive white markings and long tails with a bushy tuft at the tip. They stand or rest on their hind legs with front feet tucked against their chests, and hop on their back feet (bipedal), but walk on all fours. Kangaroo rats are seed eaters, carrying seeds to their burrows in their fur-lined cheek pouches.

Merriam's Kangaroo Rat lives in the deserts of the Southwest from western Texas to northern California. Chisel-toothed Kangaroo Rat occurs only in the far northwestern edge of Arizona. It has flattened lower incisors, hence its common name. It uses its teeth to peel off the outer layer of saltbush leaves to eat the edible interior.

Desert Kangaroo Rat is well named because it lives in the driest deserts. It gets all its water needs from the seeds and plants it eats.

Banner-tailed Kangaroo Rat is the largest kangaroo rat in Arizona, measuring over a foot long with its tail. Found in grasslands with creosotebush and mesquite, it builds large mounds approximately 12 inches (30 cm) tall and 10 feet (3 m) wide. It communicates with other Bannertails by drumming with its hind feet while sitting on top of the mounds.

Merriam's Kangaroo Rat 4½-5"

Chisel-toothed Kangaroo Rat 4¾-5"

Desert Kangaroo Rat 5-6"

Banner-tailed Kangaroo Rat 5¼-6½"

Arizona Cotton Rat
Sigmodon arizonae

Family: Rats and Mice (Muridae)

Size: L 6-8½" (15-21.5 cm); T 4-5" (10-13 cm)

Weight: 5-6 oz. (142-170 g)

Description: A large-bodied brown-to-tan rat with a dark grizzled back and rump, lighter sides and gray belly. Cream eye-ring and large dark eyes. Round ears. Short stout snout. Bicolored tail, dark gray above, lighter below, slightly shorter than head and body.

Origin/Age: native; 1-4 years

Compare: Very similar to other cotton rats, but is slightly larger and has longer hind feet. The Yellow-nosed Cotton Rat (pg. 83) has a yellow snout. Tawny-bellied (pg. 83) has a tawny belly. Hispid Cotton Rat (pg. 83) is the same size, with a shorter tail.

Habitat: wide variety from desert scrub to dense grasslands and pine forests, almost always near water or wet areas, elevations below 5,000' (1,525 m)

Home: network of tunnels, 2-3" (5-7.5 cm) wide and up to 6' (1.8 m) long, leading to inner chambers used for sleeping and feeding, often has several escape exits and dead-end tunnels for hiding

Food: herbivore; leaves, seeds, nuts

Sounds: inconsequential; high-pitched squeaks, squeals

Breeding: year-round mating; 25-27 days gestation; female can mate within hours of giving birth

Young: 2-12 (average 6) offspring up to 5 times per year; born well furred and well developed with eyes closed, eyes open at about 60 hours, able to walk and run right after birth, weaned at 1-2 weeks

Signs: nests made with plant material aboveground and below, well-worn runways in grass

Activity: nocturnal, crepuscular; active year-round, can be active on cloudy days

Tracks: hind paw 1½" (4 cm) long with a narrow heel and 5 toes, forepaw 1" (2.5 cm) long with 4 well-spread toes; often follows the same paths over and over, making individual tracks difficult to distinguish when it has been walking

Stan's Notes: One of four species of cotton rats found in Arizona, all looking very similar with a stocky body, short round snout, coarse grizzled fur and a pleasant disposition. Arizona Cotton Rat is one of the largest cotton rats and is the most common species, having the largest range in Arizona, mostly in the southeastern part of the state. There are five reported subspecies in Arizona; at least two are probably extinct.

Until recently the Arizona Cotton Rat was considered the same as Hispid Cotton Rat (pg. 83). The only difference is in chromosome number, which makes the two species nearly impossible to tell apart. Because of this, not much is known about the behaviors and reproduction of Arizona Cotton Rat, but some generalizations may be made based on its similarities to Hispid Cotton Rat.

Cotton rats can be active any time of day, depending on weather. They mark territories with scents indicating their sex, dominance and sexually readiness. They also use visual signals, such as body postures, to communicate between individuals. Females are able to breed at 40 days of age. Only the females care for the young.

Similar species on next page 81

Cotton rats are a unique group of large rodents with short round snouts and distinctive coarse fur, appearing somewhat like large voles. They live in grassy habitats, feeding mainly on green plants. In areas of activity, they make runways through the grass.

There are four cotton rat species, all of which are seen in Arizona. Yellow-nosed Cotton Rat is one of the smallest species and has an orange-to-yellow patch around its nose. The Tawny-bellied Cotton Rat has a tan or tawny belly unlike the white bellies of the other cotton rat species. The Hispid Cotton Rat has the largest range in the United States, from the Carolinas to Florida and west into the southeastern corner of Arizona.

Yellow-nosed Cotton Rat 6-7½"

Tawny-bellied Cotton Rat 6-7½"

Hispid Cotton Rat 6-8½"

White-throated Woodrat
Neotoma albigula

Family: Rats and Mice (Muridae)

Size: L 7¼-9½" (18.5-24 cm); T 6-7" (15-18 cm)

Weight: 7-7½ oz. (198-213 g)

Description: A large mouse-like rat, overall tan or gray with a white chin, chest and belly and yellow brown sides. Long pointed snout. Large ears. Large dark eyes. Tail is shorter than the body and sharply bicolored, dark above, sparsely furred, not tufted.

Origin/Age: native; 1-3 years

Compare: Mexican Woodrat (pg. 89) occurs above 5,000' (1,525 m). Bushy-tailed Woodrat (pg. 89) is much larger, with a well-furred tail. Stephen's Woodrat (pg. 89) also has a well-furred tail. The Norway Rat (pg. 91) has a naked tail with a uniform color.

Habitat: wide variety from desert scrub to coniferous and juniper forests, foothills, up to 5,000' (1,525 m)

Home: small debris pile (barely noticeable) or very large nest of many sticks, branches, bones and more (midden), interior chamber lined with dried grass and other plants, by a large cactus, tree or log or in a building, with many worn entrances, used by many rats over time but by a single rat at a time

Food: herbivore; wide variety of green plants, mainly cacti, grasses, seeds, berries, very few insects

Sounds: thumping or drumming created by the hind feet

Breeding: Jan-Sep; 25-35 days gestation

Young: 2-4 (average 3) offspring up to 3-4 times per year; born naked with eyes closed, opening at 15 days, weaned at 62-72 days

Signs: large dome-shaped stick house, reminiscent of a brush pile, containing hundreds of sticks, bark, bones and whatever else the animal is able to carry, well-worn trails leading out and away from the midden in many directions

Activity: nocturnal; active year-round, can be active on cloudy days

Tracks: hind paw 1⅜" (3.5 cm) long with a narrow heel and 5 toes, forepaw 1" (2.5 cm) long with 4 well-spread toes; frequently follows the same paths over and over, making individual tracks difficult to distinguish when it has been hopping

Stan's Notes: White-throated Woodrat is the most widespread of all species of woodrats occurring in Arizona. Often called Pack Rat because of its habit of collecting sticks, bark, bones and even shiny metal or mineral objects.

Normally nocturnal, but sometimes can be seen out and about on a cloudy day. Communicates by striking its hind feet on the ground, creating a thumping or drumming sound. Eats mainly cactus plants and fruit.

Often builds its nest underneath a particularly large prickly pear cactus, yucca or cholla. Will also nest at the base of a large tree, next to a fallen log or inside an abandoned building. Not a social animal, with only one individual or a mother with young living in each nest. Nests may be found in close proximity, however, within 30-50 feet (9.1-15 m).

Young are born with front teeth that permit them to grasp their mother's nipple and not let go. If the mother starts walking while nursing, the young will continue to clench and end up getting dragged behind her, bouncing along the ground on their backs.

midden

Additional Woodrat Species

Woodrats are large rats that look like Deer Mice (pg. 61) on steroids. They all have well-furred, bicolored tails and white hind feet. They make their homes from sticks and debris including junk from garbage, which is the reason for their other common name, Pack Rat.

All woodrats are solitary and territorial. Other woodrat species in Arizona are much more restricted in their ranges than the White-throated Woodrat. Bushy-tailed Woodrat has a fuzzy tail unlike all the other woodrats and is seen in the northern quarter of the state. Arizona Woodrat occurs in the western half of the state, usually near tributaries of the Colorado River, while Stephen's Woodrat is found in the northern half of the state. Mexican Woodrat is also seen in the northern half of Arizona, but at high elevations above 5,000 feet (1,525 m). Desert Woodrat is rare in Arizona, occurring only along the eastern border.

Arizona Woodrat 5½-6½"

Desert Woodrat 5-8¼"

Stephen's Woodrat 8¼-9"

Bushy-tailed Woodrat 8-9¾"

Mexican Woodrat 8-10"

Norway Rat
Rattus norvegicus

Family: Rats and Mice (Muridae)

Size: L 8-10" (20-25 cm); T 5-8" (13-20 cm)

Weight: ½-1 lb. (.2-.5 kg)

Description: Brown to grayish brown above and gray below. Long narrow snout. Large round ears. Dark eyes. Scaly tail, shorter than the body length.

Origin/Age: non-native; 2-4 years

Compare: Larger than all species of mice, voles and shrews. Look for large ears, a long naked tail and narrow pointed snout to help identify. Similar size as the woodrats, which all have well-furred tails. Cotton rats are smaller and have a more grizzled look.

Habitat: almost always associated with people in places such as cities, dumps, homes and farms

Home: network of interconnecting tunnels, 2-3" (5-7.5 cm) wide and up to 6' (1.8 m) long, leading to inner chambers used for sleeping and feeding, often has several escape exits and dead-end tunnels for hiding

Food: omnivore; seeds, nuts, insects, carrion, birds, bird eggs, small mammals

Sounds: high-pitched squeaks when squabbling with other rats; scratching or scampering can be heard

Breeding: year-round mating; 20-25 days gestation; female can mate within hours of giving birth

Young: 2-9 (average 6) offspring up to 10 times per year; born naked with eyes closed, eyes open at about 2 weeks, weaned at 3-4 weeks

Signs: holes chewed in barn walls or doors, well-worn paths along walls or that lead in and out of chewed holes, smell of urine near the nest site; large, hard, cylindrical, dark brown-to-black droppings, deposited along trails

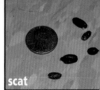
scat

Activity: nocturnal; active year-round, can be active on cloudy days

Tracks: hind paw 1½" (4 cm) long with a narrow heel and 5 toes, forepaw 1" (2.5 cm) long with 4 well-spread toes; often follows the same paths over and over, making individual tracks difficult to distinguish

Stan's Notes: A rat of cities and rural areas, greatly benefiting from its association with people. Feeds on discarded food and carrion in cities. In farm settings it eats stored food such as grain.

Also called Common Rat, Brown Rat, House Rat, Water Rat and Sewer Rat. A good swimmer and climber. Tolerates cold and hot temperatures well. Digs by loosening dirt with its front feet, pushes dirt under its belly, then turns and pushes the dirt out with its head and front feet. Chews through roots when in the way. A true omnivore and sometimes predatory, killing chickens and other small farm animals. Able to reproduce quickly when food is abundant.

Has a small territory with a high population density. Will migrate on occasion. Large numbers may leave an area, presumably in response to overcrowding and a dwindling food supply.

Scientifically described in Norway, but thought to originate from central Asia. Introduced via trading ships in the 1600-1700s.

The same species as white lab rats. A carrier of disease and fleas, it should be exterminated when possible. Hard to trap because of its escape exits. Due to intense eradication efforts (artificial selection), it has become resistant to many types of rat poisons.

Additional Rat Species

Black Rat (*R. rattus*), a species from Asia, was introduced to America in the early 1500s. Also called House Rat or Roof Rat, it is the famed species that carried bubonic plague. A climber, seen in barn rafters and running on power lines. Less common than Norway Rat and found only in the southern half of Arizona.

Black Rat
6¼-7½"

Southern Red-backed Vole
Clethrionomys gapperi

Family: Rats and Mice (Muridae)

Size: L 3-4" (7.5-10 cm); T 1-2" (2.5-5 cm)

Weight: 1-1½ oz. (28-43 g)

Description: A rusty red back with lighter brown sides. Black belly hair with white tips, making belly appear silvery white. Rounded snout. Small round ears. Small dark eyes. Short tail, bicolored and naked with a small tuft at the tip.

Origin/Age: native; 1-2 years

Compare: The Mexican Vole (pg. 99) is larger and has a shorter tail. Voles have shorter, rounder snouts and shorter tails than mice. Very limited range in Arizona, so use range to help identify.

Habitat: open wet meadows in coniferous forests, swamps, wet areas, mountain meadows, elevations up to 10,000' (3,050 m)

Home: nest with a hollow center, made of plant material, 3-4" (7.5-10 cm) wide, beneath a log or among tree roots

Food: insectivore, herbivore; insects, green leaves, fruit, seeds, leaf buds, bark of young trees, fungi

Sounds: inconsequential; rarely, if ever, heard

Breeding: late winter to late autumn mating; 17-19 days gestation

Young: 2-8 (average 5) offspring several times per year; born naked and toothless with eyes closed, body covered with fine hair and eyes open by about 12 days, weaned and on its own at about 3 weeks, appears gray until 1-2 months, then turns red

Signs: runways in grass leading beneath rocks, cut grass piled up along runways

Activity: diurnal, nocturnal; active year-round, rests and sleeps for several hours, then is active for several hours throughout the day with peaks at dawn and dusk

Tracks: hind paw ¾" (2 cm) long with 5 toes, forepaw slightly smaller with 4 toes; individual tracks are indistinguishable and create a single groove

Stan's Notes: A short-lived animal, with most living only 10-12 months; some, however, can survive to 24 months. Populations peak in autumn, with numbers dropping quickly during winter due to predation and starvation. Entire populations of birds of prey may move when vole populations drop.

Active day and night and does not hibernate. Carries on with life underneath snow at high elevations (subnivean), even expanding its home range in that environment. Will follow well-maintained surface trails only occasionally. May use tunnel systems of larger animals. Rarely enters homes or cabins. May store roots, shoots and fungi for later consumption. Underground fungi is an important and much sought food source.

Like all other vole species, the digestive tract of this species has a large pouch called a cecum, which contains microscopic bacteria (microflora). These microflora help to break down items that are hard to digest, such as cellulose, which is the chief component of green plants.

Becomes sexually mature at 5-6 months. The male will stay with the family until the young are weaned. A food staple for weasels, foxes, coyotes and many other mammals. It is also a major food item for many hawk and owl species.

Similar species on next page

All vole species in Arizona have stocky bodies, blunt noses and naked tails. They usually have dark fur and, except for the Long-tailed Vole and the Muskrat (pg. 101), they have very short tails.

Voles are considered an essential component of many ecosystems in the state, with larger mammals and birds of prey relying on healthy populations of voles as a food source. Populations rise and fall dramatically from year to year in fairly predictable cycles. Low populations of voles cause raptors and other predators to move to areas where populations are higher.

Voles occur in open areas and leave obvious signs of activity such as runways through grass, cut grass stems and piles of half-eaten grass and other plants. Most are active on the surface of the ground, retreating to underground burrows to sleep and rest. They remain active year-round even in areas of the country where winter is severe.

Mexican Vole 3¾-5½"

Montane Vole 4¼-5½"

Long-tailed Vole 4¼-5½"

Not pictured: Heather Vole 4¼-5½"

Muskrat
Ondatra zibethicus

Family: Rats and Mice (Muridae)

Size: L 8-12" (20-30 cm); T 7-12" (18-30 cm)

Weight: 1-4 lb. (.5-1.8 kg)

Description: Glossy dark brown, lighter on the sides and belly. Long naked tail, covered with scales and slightly vertically flattened (taller than it is wide). Small round ears. Tiny eyes.

Origin/Age: native; 3-10 years

Compare: Muskrat has a longer, thinner tail than American Beaver (pg. 105), which is much larger and has a large flat tail.

Habitat: ponds, lakes, ditches, small rivers, elevations up to 10,000' (3,050 m)

Home: small den, called a lodge, made of cattail leaves and other soft green (herbaceous) plant material, 1-2 underwater entrances, often has 1 chamber, sometimes a burrow in a lakeshore, larger dens may have 2 chambers with separate occupants

Food: herbivore, carnivore to a much lesser extent; aquatic plants, roots, cattail and bulrush shoots, roots and rhizomes; also eats dead fish, crayfish, clams, snails and baby birds

Sounds: inconsequential; chewing sounds can be heard when feeding above water on feeding platform

Breeding: Apr-Aug mating; 25-30 days gestation

Young: 6-7 offspring 2-3 times per year; born naked with eyes closed, swims at about 2 weeks, weaned at about 3 weeks

swimming

lodge

Signs: well-worn trails through vegetation along a lakeshore near a muskrat lodge, feeding platform made of floating plant material, 24" square (154.8 sq. cm), usually strewn with partially eaten cattails and other plants; lodge made of mud and cut vegetation, occasionally many lodges will dot the surface of a shallow lake

Activity: nocturnal, crepuscular; active all year, doesn't hibernate

Tracks: hind paw 2½-3½" (6-9 cm) long with 5 toes and a long heel, forepaw about half the size with 5 toes spread evenly; hind paws fall near or onto fore prints (direct register) when walking, often obliterating the forepaw tracks; prints may show only 4 toes since the fifth toe is not well formed, often has a tail drag mark

Stan's Notes: This animal is native only to North America, but it has been introduced all over the world. The musky odor (most evident in the male during breeding season) emanating from two glands near the base of the rat-like tail gives it the common name. Some say the common name is a derivation of the Algonquian Indian word *musquash*, which sounds somewhat like "muskrat."

Mostly aquatic, the muskrat is highly suited to living in water. It has a waterproof coat that protects it from frigid temperatures. Partially webbed hind feet and a fringe of hair along each toe help propel the animal. The tail, which is slightly flattened vertically, also helps with forward motion and is used as a rudder. Its mouth can close behind the front teeth only, allowing the animal to cut vegetation free while it is submerged.

A good swimmer that swims backward and sideways with ease. Able to stay submerged for up to 15 minutes. Surfaces to eat. May store some roots and tubers in mud below the water to consume during winter.

When small areas of a lake open up in winter, it will often sit on the ice to feed or sun itself. Although it lives in small groups, there is no social structure and individuals act mainly on their own. Becomes sexually mature the first spring after its birth.

Lodge building seems to concentrate in the fall. Not all muskrats build a mound-type lodge. Many dig a burrow in a lakeshore. A muskrat lodge is not like a beaver lodge, which is made with woody plant material. There is only one beaver lodge per lake or stream, while there are often several muskrat lodges in a body of water. Does not defecate in the lodge, so the interior living space of the lodge is kept remarkably clean.

Overcrowding can occur in fall and winter, causing individuals to travel great distances in spring to establish new homes. Many muskrats are killed when crossing roads during this season.

American Beaver
Castor canadensis

Family: Beavers (Castoridae)

Size: L 3-4' (.9-1.2 m); T 7-14" (18-36 cm)

Weight: 20-60 lb. (9-27 kg)

Description: Reddish brown fur. Body often darker than head. Large, flat, naked black tail, covered with scales. Small round ears. Large, exposed orange incisors. Tiny eyes.

Origin/Age: native; 10-15 years

Compare: Much larger than Muskrat (pg. 101), which has a long narrow tail. Look for a large flat tail to help identify the American Beaver.

Habitat: rivers, streams, ponds, lakes, ditches, elevations up to 10,000' (3,050 m) where trees and water are present

Home: den, called a lodge, hollow inside with holes on top for ventilation, 1-2 underwater entrances; beavers that live on rivers often dig burrows in riverbanks rather than constructing dens

Food: herbivore; soft bark, inner bark, aquatic plants, green leaves

Sounds: loud slap created by hitting the surface of water with the tail before diving when alarmed, chewing or gnawing sounds when feeding or felling trees

Breeding: Jan-Mar mating; 120 days gestation

Young: 1-8 kits once per year; about 1 lb. (.5 kg); born well furred with eyes open, able to swim within 1 week

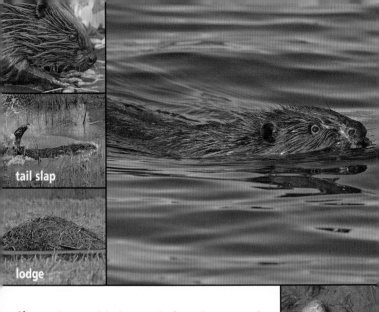

tail slap

lodge

scat

Signs: dam and lodge made from large woody branches can indicate current or former activity since structures remain well after the beaver has moved on or been killed, chewed tree trunks with large amounts of wood chips at the base of trees, flattened paths through vegetation leading to and from a lake; oval pellets, 1" (2.5 cm) long, containing sawdust-like material and bark, scat seldom on land

Activity: nocturnal, crepuscular; active year-round, even under ice and when in lodge during winter

Tracks: hind paw 5" (13 cm) long with 5 toes pointing forward and a long narrow heel, forepaw 3" (7.5 cm) with 5 splayed toes; wide tail drag mark often wipes out paw prints

Stan's Notes: Largest member of the Rodent order in Arizona. Body is well suited for swimming. Valves close off the ears and nostrils when underwater, and a clear membrane covers the eyes. Can remain submerged up to 15 minutes. Webbed toes on hind feet help it swim as fast as 6 mph (10 km/h). Special lips seal the mouth yet leave the front incisors exposed, allowing it to carry branches in its mouth without water getting inside. At the lodge, it eats the soft bark of smaller branches the same way we eat corn on the cob. Doesn't eat the interior wood. Stores branches for winter use by sticking them in mud on a lake or river bottom.

Has a specialized claw on each hind foot that is split like a comb and is used for grooming. Secretes a pungent oily substance (castor) from glands near the base of its tail. Castor is used to mark territories or boundaries called castor mounds.

Monogamous and mates for life. However, will take a new mate if partner is lost. Can live up to 20 years in captivity.

Young remain with parents through their first winter. They help cut and store a winter food source and maintain the dam while parents raise another set of young. Young disperse at two years.

Builds a dam to back up a large volume of water, creating a pond. Cuts trees at night by gnawing trunks. Uses larger branches to construct the dam and lodge. Cuts smaller branches and twigs of felled trees into 6-foot (1.8 m) sections. Dam repair is triggered by the sound of moving water, not by sight. Most repair activity takes place at night.

No other mammal besides humans changes its environment as much as beavers. Frogs, turtles and many bird species, including ducks, herons and egrets, benefit from the newly created habitat. Beaver ponds play an important role in moose populations in other areas where moose live. Moose feed on aquatic plants, cool themselves and escape biting insects in summer in beaver ponds.

Big Brown Bat
Eptesicus fuscus

Family: Bats (Vespertilionidae)

Size: L 2-3" (5-7.5 cm); T 1½-2" (4-5 cm)

Weight: ½-⁹⁄₁₀ oz. (14-26 g)

Description: Brown to yellow brown fur. Dark, membranous naked wings and tail. Lighter brown belly. Dark, oval naked ears with a short, fleshy, curved projection (tragus). Bright black eyes. Pointed snout.

Origin/Age: native; 15-20 years

Compare: A bat with few distinctive markings. Look for the uniform brown back with black ears and face to help identify. Tends to winter roost in buildings, such as homes, rather than in caves.

Habitat: wide variety such as deciduous forests, suburban areas, elevations up to 10,000' (3,050 m)

Home: walls and attics of homes, churches, barns and other buildings year-round, maternity colonies also in hollow trees, will winter in mines, tunnels and caves, but little is known about these sites

Food: insectivore; small to large flying insects

Sounds: rapid series of high-pitched clicking noises, high-pitched squeaks of pups calling persistently to mother after she leaves to feed can be heard from a distance up to 30' (9.1 m) away

Breeding: Aug-Sep mating before hibernation; 60-62 days gestation; sperm stored in the reproductive tract until the spring following mating

Young: 1-2 (usually 2) pups once per year, May to July; born breach, naked with eyes closed, weighs one-third the weight of the mother, flies at 28-35 days

109

Signs: piles of dark brown-to-black scat under roosting sites

Activity: nocturnal; active only on warm dry nights, comes out approximately 30 minutes after sunset, feeds until full, roosts the rest of night, returns to daytime roost before sunrise

scat

Tracks: none

Stan's Notes: One of nearly 30 bat species in Arizona. A common bat seen in many habitats from desert to forest, cities and the country up to 10,000 feet (3,050 m) in elevation. Found across North America from Maine to Washington and south to Florida and Central America.

Studies show that this species feeds on many crop and forest pests and insects, making it one of America's most beneficial animals and very desirable to have around. It is a fast-flying bat, reaching speeds of up to 25 mph (40 km/h), with an erratic flight pattern, evident as it swoops and dives for mosquitoes, beetles and other flying insects. Often forages over rivers and lakes, beneath street-lights or wherever large groups of flying insects congregate. Emits a high-frequency (27-48 kHz) sound (inaudible to people) to locate prey and listens for returning echoes (echolocation). Most of these bats catch and eat one insect every three seconds, consuming $\frac{1}{10}$ ounce (3 g) per hour. During summer, when rapidly growing pups demand increasing amounts of milk, a lactating female can consume up to $\frac{7}{10}$ ounce (20 g) of insects every night, which is nearly equal to her own body weight.

Rarely winters in caves, preferring to hibernate alone or in small groups. Males are generally solitary during spring and summer.

Females will gather in maternity colonies of up to 75 individuals. Loyal to these maternal roosts, females return to them year after year. Approximately 80 percent of females give birth to two pups at the maternal roosts in spring and early summer.

A mother does not carry her pups during flight, but leaves them clinging to the roost until she returns. Holds pups to her chest under a wing to nurse. Recognizes young by their vocalizations.

Homeowners frequently discover these bats when remodeling or adding onto their homes during winter months. Any unwanted bat found in homes should be professionally moved or removed to avoid hurting the animal.

Similar species on next page

Arizona has 27 species of bats, some common, others rare. All bats in Arizona eat insects and sleep during the day. Due to the air cooling at night, most species in the state are active only during the first four hours after sunset.

The Big Brown Bat is found in almost all habitats. Other species occur only in specific habitats. Arizona represents the northern limit of many species.

While some species migrate each fall, others remain in Arizona and hibernate. Some speculate there may be more species of bats moving in and out of the state that haven't been observed.

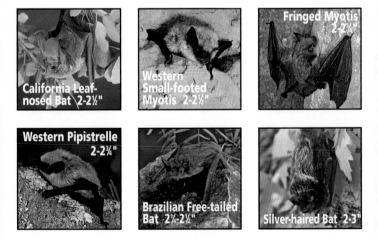

California Leaf-nosed Bat 2-2½"

Western Small-footed Myotis 2-2½"

Fringed Myotis 2-2½"

Western Pipistrelle 2-2¾"

Brazilian Free-tailed Bat 2¼-2½"

Silver-haired Bat 2-3"

California Myotis 2-3"

Townsend's Big-eared Bat 2¼-3"

Spotted Bat 2½-3"

Yuma Myotis 2½-3"

Arizona Myotis 2¾-3"

Southwestern Myotis 2¾-3"

Long-eared Myotis 2¾-3"

Allen's Big-eared Bat 2¾-3"

Hoary Bat 2-4"

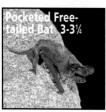

Pocketed Free-tailed Bat 3-3¼

Lesser Long-nosed Bat 3-3¼"

Mexican Long-tongued Bat 3-3½"

Similar species on next page 113

Long-legged Myotis 3-3½"

Western Red Bat 3¼-3¾"

Cave Myotis 3½-4"

Pallid Bat 3¾-4"

Western Yellow Bat 3¾-4"

Big Free-tailed Bat 4¼-5½"

Western Mastiff Bat 5-5¼"

Underwood's Mastiff Bat 5½-6"

Least Chipmunk

Tamias minimus

Family: Squirrels (Sciuridae)

Size: L 3-4" (7.5-10 cm); T 3-4" (7.5-10 cm)

Weight: 2-2¼ oz. (57-64 g)

Description: Overall brown fur with alternating dark and light stripes from nose to base of tail. Orange brown sides with a lighter brown rump. Chin, chest and belly are pale white to gray. Long orange brown tail, nearly the length of the body, usually with a thin dark line running the entire length.

Origin/Age: native; 2-4 years

Compare: The Cliff Chipmunk (pg. 129) has a lighter back with much less distinct side (lateral) stripes. Other chipmunks (pp. 121-137) look similar, so use the range maps to help identify.

Habitat: rocky outcrops, cliffs, roadsides, open coniferous forests, up to 10,000' (3,050 m) and higher

Home: burrow, entrance usually a small round hole with no trace of excavated dirt, sometimes at the base of a rock, occasionally nests in a tree, may have different burrows in summer and winter, winter burrow is deeper underground

Food: omnivore; seeds, fruit, nuts, insects, fungi, buds, flowers, frogs, baby birds, bird eggs, small snakes

Sounds: series of distinctive high-pitched "chip" notes that sound like a small bird, similar to most other chipmunk species

Breeding: Mar-May mating; 28-30 days gestation

Young: up to 7 offspring 1-2 times per year; born naked with eyes closed, weaned at about 60 days

117

Signs: piles of cracked seeds and acorns and other food on a log or large rock; oblong dark brown pellets, ⅛" (.3 cm) long, often not seen and not key in identifying this species

Activity: diurnal; does not come out on cold, rainy days

Tracks: hind paw ¾"-1¼" (2-3 cm) long with 5 toes, forepaw with 4 toes is about half the size of hind paw; 1 set of 4 tracks; hind paws fall in front of fore prints; tracks rarely seen since it lives in a dry rocky habitat and usually does not come out from burrow when snow is on the ground

Stan's Notes: This is the smallest and most widespread of the 22 chipmunk species seen in North America. One of six chipmunk species in Arizona. Ranges across the western half of the United States, extending north up the Rocky Mountains of Canada, across Canada eastward, dropping down into some northern states such as Minnesota and Wisconsin. Home range is estimated at ¼ acre (.1 ha) with overlapping boundaries. It occurs in isolated pockets in Arizona in northern and eastern parts of the state.

Like the other chipmunks, this one has fur-lined internal cheek pouches for carrying food, dirt and other items while it excavates tunnels. Often runs with its tail held vertically, like the antenna of a dune buggy. When it is on a sun-dappled forest floor or in a rocky habitat, the bold stripes provide a great camouflage.

Comfortable climbing trees to gather seeds, buds and flowers for food. Stores large amounts of seeds, nuts and dried berries in an underground cavity. Feeds on its cache when it can't get outside due to weather. Known to steal food from neighboring "chippie" caches. One study has reported that nearly 500 acorns and 1,000 cherry pits were found in a Least Chipmunk cache.

Can become tame and even very bold, seeking people for hand-outs in areas with increased human contact. Lives in association with Colorado Chipmunks (pg. 125) without apparent conflict.

Doesn't add a thick layer of fat in preparation for winter. Instead, it caches food and sleeps for 1-2 weeks at a time, waking to feed. Drifts into a state of deep sleep called torpor, which includes a mild metabolic rate drop, but not to the level of true hibernation.

Matures sexually at 10-12 months. Breeding season begins in late March or early April and lasts only a few weeks, depending on elevation. In high elevations, breeding season may start as late as July. Female can have up to two litters each breeding season, but this is not common.

Hopi Chipmunk
Tamias rufus

Family: Squirrels (Sciuridae)

Size: L 3¼-4" (8-10 cm); T 3-4" (7.5-10 cm)

Weight: 2-2¼ oz. (57-64 g)

Description: Pale gray to pale orange. Indistinct darker orange and white stripes on back (dorsal) from shoulders to rump. Dark orange stripe through eyes. Gray cheeks. White chin, chest, belly, nearly white feet, often a white spot behind ears. Long tail, nearly the length of body, orange to brown, black-tipped.

Origin/Age: native; 2-4 years

Compare: Colorado Chipmunk (pg. 125) has more distinct dorsal stripes. The Cliff Chipmunk (pg. 129) is overall darker and has a fluffier tail. Look for the pale gray fur and indistinct stripes on the back of the Hopi Chipmunk. Seen only in northeastern Arizona, so use range to help identify.

Habitat: canyons, rocky outcrops, cliffs, juniper and other forests, elevations up to 7,000' (2,135 m)

Home: burrow, small round entrance hole with no trace of excavated dirt, may have summer and winter burrows, winter burrow is deeper underground

Food: omnivore; seeds, fruit, nuts, insects, fungi, buds, flowers, carrion

Sounds: series of high-pitched "chips" given while flipping its tail, most chipmunk species sound similar

Breeding: Feb-Mar mating; 30-33 days gestation

Young: 2-6 offspring once per year; born naked with eyes closed, eyes open at 30 days, emerges at 40 days, weaned at 55 days, mature at 11 months

121

Signs: piles of open seeds at favorite feeding spots on prominent rocks and logs; oblong dark brown pellets, ⅛" (.3 cm) long, often not seen and not key in identifying this species

Activity: diurnal; most active in midmorning and midafternoon, seen running over and along large rocks; does not come out on cold, rainy days

Tracks: hind paw 1¼" (3 cm) long with 5 toes, forepaw with 4 toes is about half the size of hind paw; 1 set of 4 tracks; hind paws fall in front of fore prints; tracks rarely seen since it lives in a dry rocky habitat and usually does not come out from burrow when snow is on the ground

Stan's Notes: By far the most pale of the six chipmunk species in Arizona. Range is restricted to northeastern Arizona. Seems to prefer broken rocks or rubble at the base of cliffs (talus fields) and does not range far from these areas. Active from late February through November, making it the most active chipmunk species in Arizona.

Was once considered the same species as Colorado Chipmunk (pg. 125), but these species apparently do not interbreed where their ranges overlap.

Highly associated with coniferous forests, especially juniper and pinyon, feeding heavily on cones and seeds. Stuffs its cheeks full and runs to a feeding spot, usually high rocks, where it can see in all directions while feeding. Collects and stores many items of food for winter consumption. Like other chipmunks, the Hopi has fur-lined internal cheek pouches for carrying food and other items, such as dirt, while it excavates tunnels.

Comfortable climbing trees or steep cliffs. Holds tail horizontally when running, which can help to identify. However, field marks, range and elevation should also be considered.

Colorado Chipmunk

Tamias quadrivittatus

Family: Squirrels (Sciuridae)

Size: L 3½-4¼" (9-10.5 cm); T 3½-4" (9-10 cm)

Weight: 2-2½ oz. (57-71 g)

Description: Overall orange to brown with alternating light and dark stripes from the nose almost to the base of tail. Orange brown sides and gray rump. Chin, chest and belly are white to gray. Long, darker brown tail, same length as the body.

Origin/Age: native; 2-4 years

Compare: The Least Chipmunk (pg. 117) is more common, slightly smaller and has stripes going all the way to the base of its tail. Cliff Chipmunk (pg. 129), which is much more common in Arizona and more widespread, is slightly larger with much less distinct stripes on its back (dorsal) and sides.

Habitat: rocky outcrops, canyons, foothills, dry and open forests, elevations up to 10,500' (3,200 m)

Home: burrow, small round entrance hole with no trace of excavated dirt, sometimes nests in a tree, may have different burrows in summer and winter, winter burrow is deeper underground

Food: omnivore; seeds, fruit, nuts, insects, fungi, buds, flowers, carrion

Sounds: series of distinctive high-pitched "chip" notes that sound like most other chipmunk species

Breeding: Apr-May mating; 30-33 days gestation

Young: 4-7 offspring once per year; born naked with eyes closed, weaned at about 42-49 days

Signs: piles of cracked seeds and acorns and other food on a log or large rock; oblong dark brown pellets, ⅛" (.3 cm) long, often not seen and not key in identifying this species

scat

Activity: diurnal; active in late morning and again in afternoon, does not come out on cold, rainy days or during winter

Tracks: hind paw 1¼" (3 cm) long with 5 toes, forepaw with 4 toes is about half the size of hind paw; 1 set of 4 tracks; hind paws fall in front of fore prints; tracks rarely seen since it lives in a dry rocky habitat and usually does not come out from burrow when snow is on the ground

Stan's Notes: One of the smaller chipmunks species in Arizona. Ranges only in the far northeastern corner of the state in a very limited range. Home range is estimated to be 1 acre (.4 ha) with overlapping boundaries. Some studies show this species travels up to 5 acres (2 ha).

Like the other chipmunks, the Colorado Chipmunk has fur-lined internal cheek pouches for carrying food and other items, such as dirt, while it excavates tunnels. Often runs holding its tail in a horizontal position unlike the Least Chipmunk (pg. 117), which holds its tail vertically. Identifying the Colorado Chipmunk just by tail position is difficult, but noting it can be helpful.

Climbs trees more than other chipmunk species to gather seeds, buds and flowers for food. Stores small amounts of seeds, nuts and dried berries in an underground cavity. Feeds on its cache when it cannot get outside due to inclement weather.

Can become tame and even very bold, seeking people for hand-outs in areas with increased human contact. Often lives in close association with other chipmunks with no apparent conflict.

Does not add a thick layer of fat in preparation for winter. Caches food instead and sleeps for 1-2 weeks at a time, waking to feed. Drifts into a state of deep sleep called torpor, which includes a mild metabolic rate drop, but not to the level of true hibernation.

Cliff Chipmunk
Tamias dorsalis

Family: Squirrels (Sciuridae)

Size: L 4¼-5½" (10.5-14 cm); T 3¼-5" (8-13 cm)

Weight: 2-3 oz. (57-85 g)

Description: Overall gray to tan with faint stripes on the back (dorsal). Distinct white stripes above and below eyes. Dark eye line. Gray cheeks, sides and feet. Pale white chin, chest and belly. Long, fluffy, dark gray tail, nearly the length of the body.

Origin/Age: native; 2-4 years

Compare: The other chipmunks (pp. 117-137) have more distinct stripes on their sides and back. Look for the gray sides and indistinct stripes to identify the Cliff Chipmunk. Occurs in a diagonal band across Arizona and is fairly common, so also use range to help identify.

Habitat: rocky outcrops, cliffs, roadsides, coniferous forests, elevations up to 9,000' (2,745 m)

Home: burrow, often under rocks or in cliff faces, small round entrance hole with no excavated dirt, winter burrow is deeper than summer burrow

Food: omnivore; seeds, fruit, nuts, insects, fungi, buds, flowers, carrion

Sounds: series of distinctive high-pitched barks (up to 100 times per minute) given while flipping its tail, most chipmunk species sound similar

Breeding: Apr-May mating; 28-30 days gestation

Young: 4-8 offspring once per year; born naked with eyes closed, emerges from burrow at 35-45 days, weaned at about 60 days

Signs: piles of cracked seeds and acorns and other food on a log or large rock; oblong dark brown pellets, ⅛" (.3 cm) long, often not seen and not key in identifying this species

Activity: diurnal; does not come out on cold, rainy days

Tracks: hind paw 1¼" (3 cm) long with 5 toes, forepaw with 4 toes is about half the size of hind paw; 1 set of 4 tracks; hind paws fall in front of fore prints; tracks rarely seen since it lives in a dry rocky habitat and usually does not come out from burrow when snow is on the ground

Stan's Notes: This chipmunk has indistinct stripes, but inhabits dry open areas where more bold striping for camouflage is not as important as it would be in other habitats. The most common of the chipmunks in Arizona, ranging in a large band across the state. Home range is estimated to be ¼ acre (.1 ha) with overlapping boundaries. Distribution is from Arizona, Nevada, Colorado and western New Mexico down into Mexico.

Like the other chipmunk species, the Cliff has fur-lined internal cheek pouches for carrying food, dirt and other items while it excavates tunnels. Groups of females may gather food together, traveling short distances and returning home with cheeks stuffed with seeds, nuts or berries.

Comfortable climbing trees to gather seeds, buds and flowers for food. Stores large amounts of seeds, nuts and dried berries in an underground cavity. Feeds on its cache when it can't get outside due to weather.

Does not add a thick layer of fat in preparation for winter. Drifts into a state of deep sleep known as torpor, which includes a mild metabolic rate drop, but not to the level of true hibernation. Sleeps for 1-2 weeks at a time, waking to feed on its cache.

Matures sexually at 10-12 months. Breeding season begins in late April or May. Young emerge from burrows at 35-45 days of age.

Uinta Chipmunk
Tamias umbrinus

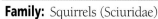

Family: Squirrels (Sciuridae)

Size: L 4¾-5¼" (12-13.5 cm); T 3-4½" (7.5-11 cm)

Weight: 2-3 oz. (57-85 g)

Description: Overall light brown to brown with alternating distinct dark and white stripes from shoulders to base of tail. Stripe through both eyes, not as dark as stripes on the back. Gray cheeks. White chin, chest and belly. Nearly white feet. Long brown tail, lighter on the underside and black-tipped.

Origin/Age: native; 2-4 years

Compare: Least Chipmunk (pg. 117) is more grayish, has gray undersides and runs with tail held vertically. More brown than other chipmunks. Look for the dark stripes and also use range to help identify.

Habitat: variety of habitats from pinyon-juniper forests to shrublands, river bottoms, forest edges, talus slopes, mountains, canyons, rocky outcrops, between 6,500-12,000' (1,980-3,660 m)

Home: burrow, beneath rocks, logs and shrubs, several entrances, small round entrance holes, no excavated dirt, winter burrow is deeper underground

Food: omnivore; seeds, fruit, nuts, insects, fungi, buds, flowers, carrion

Sounds: series of high-pitched "chips" given while flipping its tail, most chipmunk species sound similar

Breeding: Mar-Apr mating; 30-32 days gestation

Young: 2-6 offspring once per year; born naked with eyes closed, eyes open at 30 days, emerges at 40 days, weaned at about 55 days, mature at 11 months

Signs: piles of open seeds at favorite feeding spots on prominent rocks and logs; oblong dark brown pellets, ⅛" (.3 cm) long, often not seen and not key in identifying this species

Activity: diurnal; active most of the day, does not come out on cold, rainy days or during very hot days

Tracks: hind paw 1¼" (3 cm) long with 5 toes, forepaw with 4 toes is about half the size of hind paw; 1 set of 4 tracks; hind paws fall in front of fore prints

Stan's Notes: One of the least studied of the chipmunks. Occurs in a very limited range in the state. Lives in north central Arizona, occupying pinyon and juniper forests, spending more time in the forest than the other chipmunk species.

Found in parts of eight western states. Unlike the usually uniform and continuous population distributions of other chipmunks, the range of the Uinta is broken into pockets of isolated populations. Has a small home range of 2 acres (.8 ha).

Seems to get along with other chipmunk species. Especially tame at campgrounds, where it is known to beg for food.

Climbs trees or steep cliffs easily. Carries tail horizontally when running, which can help to identify, but range, elevation and field marks should also be considered. Has fur-lined internal cheek pouches to carry food, dirt and other items while it digs tunnels.

Caches food for winter consumption and also puts on a layer of fat, which aids in hibernation. Still, it wakes periodically during winter to feed on stored food before returning to hibernation.

Gray-collared Chipmunk
Tamias cinereicollis

Family: Squirrels (Sciuridae)

Size: L 4¾-5¼" (12-13.5 cm); T 3-4½" (7.5-11 cm)

Weight: 2-3 oz. (57-85 g)

Description: Overall brown fur with alternating dark and light stripes from nose to base of tail. Orange brown sides with a lighter brown rump. Distinctive gray cheeks, neck, shoulders and chin. Long orange brown tail, nearly the length of the body, usually with a thin dark line running the entire length.

Origin/Age: native; 2-4 years

Compare: Least Chipmunk (pg. 117) lacks the gray cheeks, neck and shoulders. Cliff Chipmunk (pg. 129) occurs at lower elevations and has less distinct black stripes on its back. Best to use location and elevation to help identify this species.

Habitat: dry, open pine, fir and other coniferous woods at 6,500-11,000' (1,830-3,355 m)

Home: burrow, entrance usually a small round hole with no trace of excavated dirt, sometimes by a rock, occasionally nests in a tree or old woodpecker hole, may have different burrows in summer and winter, winter burrows are deeper underground

Food: omnivore; seeds, fruit, nuts, insects, fungi, buds, flowers, frogs, baby birds, bird eggs, small snakes

Sounds: distinctive high-pitched series of "chip" notes that sound like a small bird

Breeding: Apr-May mating; 28-30 days gestation

Young: 4-6 offspring 1-2 times per year; born naked with eyes closed, weaned at about 40-45 days

137

Signs: piles of peeled cones and acorns and other seeds on a log or large rock; oblong dark brown pellets, ⅛" (.3 cm) long, often not seen and not key in identifying this species

Activity: diurnal; doesn't come out on cold rainy days, apparently sometimes active during winter, leaving tracks in the snow

Tracks: hind paw 1¼" (3 cm) long with 5 toes, forepaw with 4 toes is about half the size of hind paw; 1 set of 4 tracks; hind paws fall in front of fore prints; tracks rarely seen since it lives in a dry rocky habitat, but tracks can sometimes be seen in the snow

Stan's Notes: Not a common chipmunk species, found mostly in coniferous forests in high elevations, restricted to the mountains of central Arizona and southwestern New Mexico. Whether it is on a sun-dappled forest floor or in a rocky habitat, its bold stripes provide great camouflage. It sports a distinctive gray collar, hence the common name "Gray-collared" and species name *cinereicollis*.

Like the other chipmunks, this one has fur-lined internal cheek pouches for carrying food and also dirt and other items while it digs tunnels. Feeds mainly on Douglas Fir and Ponderosa Pine cone seeds, but also consumes acorns and berries. Comfortable climbing trees to gather seeds, buds and flowers for food. Most spend the day foraging for seeds and cones on the forest floor or climbing trees.

Usually solitary. Most active in early morning and late afternoon. Sometimes makes its home in an old woodpecker cavity. Stores large amounts of seeds, nuts and dried berries in an underground cavity. Feeds on its cache when it is not outside due to weather. One of the few chipmunk species that can be seen during winter. Hibernates for short periods of time, waking to feed, and can be also seen aboveground on warm, sunny winter days.

In late winter the males emerge several weeks before the females. Once the females emerge, mating follows shortly afterward. Males will compete for females, but both males and females mate with several mates per season.

The home range or territory is approximately ¼-½ acre (.1-2 ha), with parts of one territory overlapping onto others. Males have larger territories than the females.

Matures sexually at 10-12 months. Breeding season is later than most other chipmunk species, beginning in late April and early May and lasting only a few weeks. Female has only one litter per season, which is uncommon since most chipmunk species have two in a season.

White-tailed Antelope Squirrel
Ammospermophilus leucurus

Family: Squirrels (Sciuridae)

Size: L 5½-7½" (14-19 cm); T 2-3½" (5-9 cm)

Weight: 3¾-5 oz. (106-142 g)

Description: Overall reddish brown to gray with a white side stripe from the shoulder to hip. Paler undersides. Small short ears. Small bushy tail, white below, black or dark gray on top, with a dark tip.

Origin/Age: native; 1-5 years

Compare: The Golden-mantled Ground Squirrel (pg. 161) has dark side stripes and rusty red shoulders, nape and head. Chipmunks (pp. 117-137) have striped faces.

Habitat: semideserts, shrublands, pinyon-juniper woodlands, dry rocky areas, elevations below 7,000' (2,135 m)

Home: burrow, up to 10' (3 m) long, several feet deep, no excess dirt at entrance, entrance often under shrubs or exposed, chamber lined with leaves, dried grass and bark, also uses rock crevices and abandoned animal burrows, has short escape tunnels with no chambers for emergencies only

Food: omnivore; green plants, seeds, insects, carrion, lizards, mice

Sounds: usually silent, but gives a high-pitched alarm trill

Breeding: Feb-Apr mating; 30-35 days gestation

Young: 5-11 offspring once per year in April or May; born naked with eyes closed, independent after weaning, seen aboveground by about 5-6 weeks

Signs: small round entrance holes under shrubs, worn path to and from the burrow; scat is rarely seen

Activity: diurnal; most active in early morning and again in late afternoon, but can be seen during the middle of the day, usually seen running quickly back and forth to the burrow with tail held over its back, becomes much less active during long hot spells, also becomes inactive during cold, snowy parts of winter

Tracks: hind paw 1½" (4 cm) long with 5 toes, forepaw ¾" (2 cm) long with 4 toes; tracks usually seen around burrow entrance in dry sandy soils and dirt

Stan's Notes: Called White-tailed Antelope Squirrel due to the flashy white underside of its tail, similar to that of a much larger mammal, the Pronghorn Antelope (not shown). Runs very fast, like an antelope, carrying its tail over its rump. Almost always holds its tail over its back.

One of the most widespread of antelope squirrels in southwestern states. Ranges across northern Arizona northward into Utah, Colorado and Nevada. Seen only in northern parts of Arizona in elevations below 7,000 feet (2,135 m).

Home range is up to 3 acres (1.2 ha), with daily travels covering less than half that area. Seldom sits still. Instead, it races around its territory, gathering food and nesting material and returning to its burrow. Feeds on green vegetation, seeds, insects, small lizards and occasionally on smaller mammals. Digs its own burrow or takes residency in the burrow of other ground-dwelling species such as kangaroo rats or other ground squirrels.

Tolerates heat much better than cold. Spreads out on the floor of its burrow with its sparsely furred belly on the earth to cool itself. When out of the burrow, it also seeks shade during hot periods of the day.

Most active during morning and again in late afternoon. Becomes inactive in very hot or cold weather. Suns itself on rocks during winter. Retreats to its burrow in extremely cold weather, but it is thought not to hibernate.

Harris's Antelope Squirrel
Ammospermophilus harrisii

Family: Squirrels (Sciuridae)

Size: L 6¼-7" (15.5-18 cm); T 2½-3½" (6-9 cm)

Weight: 3½-4½ oz. (99-128 g)

Description: Overall reddish brown to gray with a white side stripe from the shoulder to hip. Paler undersides. Small short ears. White ring around eyes. Bushy tail, peppered black and white, with a darker tip, often held over the back.

Origin/Age: native; 1-5 years

Compare: Golden-mantled Ground Squirrel (pg. 161) has dark side stripes and rust red shoulders, nape and head. Chipmunks (pp. 117-137) have striped faces. White-tailed Antelope Squirrel (pg. 141) has a white undertail and is in northern Arizona.

Habitat: deserts, semideserts, shrublands, dry rocky areas, elevations below 4,000' (1,220 m)

Home: burrow, up to 10' (3 m) long, several feet deep, no excess dirt at entrance, entrance often under shrubs or exposed, chamber lined with leaves, dried grass and bark, also uses rock crevices and abandoned animal burrows, has short escape tunnels with no chambers for emergencies only

Food: omnivore; green plants, seeds, insects, carrion, lizards, mice

Sounds: high-pitched alarm trill, chitters when running

Breeding: Dec-Feb mating; 30-33 days gestation

Young: 5-9 offspring once per year in April or May; born naked with eyes closed, independent after weaning, seen aboveground by about 5-6 weeks

145

juvenile

Signs: small round entrance holes under shrubs, often mesquite or creosotebush, worn path to and from burrow; scat rarely seen

Activity: diurnal; most active in early morning and again in late afternoon, but can be seen during the middle of the day, usually seen running quickly back and forth to the burrow with tail held over its back, becomes inactive during cold parts of winter

Tracks: hind paw 1¼" (3 cm) long with 5 toes, forepaw ¾" (2 cm) long with 4 toes; tracks usually seen around burrow entrance in dry sandy soils and dirt

Stan's Notes: A true ground squirrel. Also known as Gray-tailed Antelope Squirrel, Yuma Antelope Ground Squirrel and Marmot Squirrel. Often seen in backyards and around bird feeders in the suburbs in the southern half of Arizona. Can carry large amounts of food in its cheek pouches. Gathers and feeds on a variety of different kinds of seeds, such as mesquite beans, which its shells before storing. Eats many types of cactus fruit. Often climbs the thorniest cactus to gather the fruit or will use it as a high point to look for danger.

Extreme desert heat does not seem to bother this squirrel in the way it affects other desert critters. Stays active all summer, even during the hottest part of the day, by maintaining a higher body temperature than the other mammals, from 97-107°F (36-42°C). Apparently it obtains most of its water from the food it has eaten. Does not hibernate and therefore doesn't have any extra body fat, resulting in very little body weight change throughout the year.

Often seen running with its tail held straight up in the air. When at rest, holds the tail over its back. Gives a high-pitched trill when alarmed and will often stomp its feet and give a chittering call just before bolting down into its burrow. Lives in a burrow it has dug itself. Usually solitary except for mothers with young.

The coloration of the fur helps this squirrel blend in with the desert environment. Individuals can be highly variable in pattern and color. Young appear scruffy with less defined markings than the adults. Males and females look the same and are the same size. They molt twice each year, the first time in May and June into a lightweight summer coat, and again in October and November into heavier fur. The young tend to be slightly smaller at first, but quickly obtain adult size and coloring.

The genus name *Ammospermophilus* comes from *ammos* ("sand"), *spermotos* ("seed") and *philos* ("loving" or "desiring"). The species name *harrisii* honors Edward Harris.

Spotted Ground Squirrel
Spermophilus spilosoma

Family: Squirrels (Sciuridae)

Size: L 5-8½" (13-21.5 cm); T 2-3½" (5-9 cm)

Weight: 3-5 oz. (85-142 g)

Description: Overall gray to brown with many faint whitish spots, more pronounced on the hind quarter of back. White-to-tan belly. Small round ears that don't stand erect. Short thin tail, covered with hair, often with a dark tip.

Origin/Age: native; 1-4 years

Compare: Chipmunks (pp. 117-137) are smaller and have striping on their bodies and faces. White-tailed Antelope Squirrel (pg. 141) is a similar size, but lacks spots. Harris's Antelope Squirrel (pg. 145) has a white stripe on its sides and lacks any spots.

Habitat: dry grasslands, sandy soils, grazed fields, desert scrub, low elevations below 5,000' (1,525 m)

Home: burrow, up to 20' (6.1 m) long, several feet deep, no excess dirt at the entrance, burrow system has many side tunnels and chambers and several entrances, main entrance is often under shrubs, chambers are lined with leaves and dried grass

Food: omnivore; mainly green plants; also eats seeds, lizards, baby mice, insects and carrion

Sounds: high-pitched trill; will rapidly stomp its hind feet

Breeding: Apr-May mating; 27-28 days gestation

Young: 5-12 offspring 1-2 times per year; born naked with eyes closed, seen aboveground by about 4-5 weeks

Signs: small round entrance holes under shrubs, well-worn path to and from the burrow or to a secondary burrow

Activity: diurnal; active during midday with peak activity in late morning and late afternoon, usually seen running quickly back and forth to burrow, often standing upright in fields and meadows

Tracks: hind paw 1¼" (3 cm) long with 5 toes, forepaw ½" (1 cm) long with 4 toes; tracks usually seen around burrow entrance in dry sandy soils and dirt

Stan's Notes: An uncommon, but widespread ground squirrel in Arizona that is shy and secretive. Often unnoticed by the average observer. Usually associated with sparsely vegetated habitat such as desert scrub. Ranges from the southern edge of South Dakota to the eastern edge of Colorado, through most of New Mexico to western Texas and west into northern and southeastern Arizona.

Prefers deep sandy soils with sparse vegetation and seems to be associated with silvery wormwood, a common shrubby plant. Less omnivorous than other ground squirrels, but still consumes a fair amount of insects, lizards and any carrion it can find.

Males have larger home ranges than females, from ¼-1 acre (.1-.4 ha). Maintains several burrows, which it excavates itself, often having a well-worn path on the ground between the burrows and 2-3 entrance holes at the base of a shrub. Lives in small groups with burrows spaced apart.

Breeding begins in mid-April and May, with young born about a month later and emerging from their burrow in July and August. Family groups often gather around the burrow entrance. When feeling threatened, individuals will stomp their feet before diving down the hole for safety.

One study showed that the aboveground activities of the Spotted Ground Squirrel typically are feeding and foraging (66 percent), altered behavior such as standing and looking about (15 percent), investigating (6 percent) and sunbathing, grooming and other behaviors (8 percent). Active all year in areas of its range where winter is not severe.

Round-tailed Ground Squirrel
Spermophilus tereticaudus

Family: Squirrels (Sciuridae)

Size: L 6½-7" (16-18 cm); T 2-4½" (5-11 cm)

Weight: 4-6 oz. (113-170 g)

Description: Long, narrow tan-to-gray body with little to no distinguishing markings. Paler below. Very small round ears. Large dark eyes with a white eye-ring. Short legs. Long, thin hairy tail, appearing round and well furred.

Origin/Age: native; 1-4 years

Compare: Similar size as Spotted Ground Squirrel (pg. 149), which has faint white spots. All the chipmunks (pp. 117-137) have stripes. Much smaller than the prairie dogs (pp. 185-189).

Habitat: fields, pastures, grasslands, along roads and parking lots, cemeteries, below 4,000' (1,220 m)

Home: burrow, up to 20' (6.1 m) long and often only several feet deep, with a hibernation chamber beneath the frost line and no excess dirt at the entrance, many side tunnels and several entrance and exit holes; will plug entrances and exits each night with plant material

Food: omnivore; green plants, seeds, insects, carrion

Sounds: high-pitched single note whistles when alarmed or threatened

Breeding: Jan-Feb mating; 25-35 days gestation

Young: 6-12 offspring once per year in May; born naked with eyes closed, becomes independent after it is weaned, seen aboveground by about 5-6 weeks

Signs: small round entrance holes in grass, runways 2" (5 cm) wide worn in grass (made by its low-slung body and short legs) leading to and from the holes; scat is rarely seen since the animal often defecates in its burrow or in tall grass

Activity: diurnal; most active a couple of hours after sunrise and through midday, retires to its burrow 1-2 hours before sunset, does not come out on cold, windy or rainy days

Tracks: hind paw 1½" (4 cm) long with 5 toes, forepaw 1 (2.5 cm) long with 4 toes; tracks usually seen around burrow entrance

Stan's Notes: A plain-looking small ground squirrel that lives in the deserts of the Southwest, ranging from southern California through half of Arizona and down into Mexico. It inhabits sandy soils of desert scrub and has adapted well to human development, often scampering along roads and parking lots.

Semisocial, which is a fairly unusual behavior in this mammal group. Often seen in small colonies, with individuals interacting with each other aboveground. Females construct and maintain their own burrows for giving birth and raising young. Young are often seen together near the burrow entrance at about 5-6 weeks of age. Males build and maintain their own burrows.

This squirrel has two periods of activity every day, once in the morning and again in late afternoon. Often active all day long on cloudy or overcast days, when midday temperatures are not as hot. When active it spends up to 50 percent of its time foraging for food on the ground.

Feeds mainly on plants and seeds, often climbing into a shrub or tree to eat the leaves or gather some seeds. Just as comfortable gathering food on the ground. Green plants make up most of the diet during spring and summer, while in winter the diet consists mainly of seeds. Will eat insects if available.

Communicates with a high-pitched whistle that sends the other squirrels running into their burrows. Females give warning calls more than the males and usually live in closer proximity to other females than males. Females tend to be dominant from March to April, while males are dominant from January to March.

Not a true hibernator, going into a light hibernation called torpor during a few months in November and December, emerging in January and February to mate. Fur color has a paler appearance during summer than in winter.

Thirteen-lined Ground Squirrel
Spermophilus tridecemlineatus

Family: Squirrels (Sciuridae)

Size: L 6-8" (15-20 cm); T 2-5" (5-13 cm)

Weight: 4-9 oz. (113-255 g)

Description: Long, narrow brown body with 13 alternating tan and dark brown stripes from nape to base of tail. Small tan spots in the dark stripes. Short round ears. Large dark eyes. Short legs. Thin hairy tail, one-third the length of body.

Origin/Age: native; 1-3 years

Compare: Larger than the Least Chipmunk (pg. 117), which lacks spots on its stripes and has stripes on its face. The Spotted Ground Squirrel (pg. 149) has a similar size and faint white spots. Consider the range since the Thirteen-lined Ground Squirrel is seen only in parts of eastern Arizona.

Habitat: fields, pastures, grasslands, by roads, cemeteries

Home: burrow, up to 20' (6.1 m) long and often only several feet deep, with a hibernation chamber beneath the frost line and no excess dirt at the entrance, many side tunnels and several entrance and exit holes; will plug entrances and exits each night with plant material

Food: omnivore; green plants, seeds, insects, bird eggs, baby mice

Sounds: trill-like whistles when threatened or alarmed

Breeding: usually April mating; 27-28 days gestation

Young: 6-12 offspring once per year in May; born naked with eyes closed, becomes independent after it is weaned, seen aboveground by about 6 weeks

juveniles

Signs: small round entrance holes in grass, runways 2" (5 cm) wide worn in grass (made by its low-slung body and short legs) leading to and from the holes; scat is rarely seen since the animal often defecates in its burrow or in tall grass

Activity: diurnal; most active a couple of hours after sunrise and through midday, retires to its burrow 1-2 hours before sunset, does not come out on cold, windy or rainy days, rarely comes out when snow is on the ground

Tracks: hind paw 1½" (4 cm) long with 5 toes, forepaw 1 (2.5 cm) long with 4 toes; tracks usually seen around burrow entrance

Stan's Notes: Not a gopher, but sometimes called Striped Gopher. Also called Federation Squirrel due to the pattern of stripes with spots on its body that resemble the U.S. Stars and Stripes.

When there is frequent human contact at places such as roadside rest areas and golf courses, it can be friendly and is usually tame. Semisocial, interacting with other ground squirrels during the day when feeding. Individuals have separate burrows, but live in large colonies. Colonies are not highly organized and may result from a reduction in available habitat.

A fast runner, reaching speeds up to 8 mph (13 km/h). Zigzags and turns back when pursued. Stands upright to survey its territory. Gives a trill-like whistle at the first sign of danger and runs quickly to the main burrow or one of its short, dead-end escape burrows. Often stays inside the entrance, poking its head out, repeating its alarm call.

Genus name *Spermophilus* means "seed lover." Stores some seeds in burrow for cold or rainy days. When insects are abundant, eats more insects than plants. Adds enough body fat in summer to start hibernating in September or October. Often enters hibernation sooner than chipmunks and emerges later, making it one of the longest true hibernators in Arizona. Does not wake to feed, like chipmunks. Rolls up into a ball in the hibernation chamber. Heart rate, body temperature and respiration drop dramatically. Reduced heart rate and respiration conserve energy in winter, but still loses up to half its body weight by spring.

Male emerges from hibernation before female. Mating occurs just after female emerges, usually in April. The short breeding season may explain why the female has only one litter each year. After mating, the male does not participate in raising young.

Young often do not disperse far and dig their own burrows near their mother. This substantially increases the colony size.

Golden-mantled Ground Squirrel
Spermophilus lateralis

Family: Squirrels (Sciuridae)

Size: L 7-9½" (18-24 cm); T 2½-4¾" (6-12 cm)

Weight: 6-14 oz. (170-397 g)

Description: Overall brown with a gray back. Red orange head, neck and shoulders with white and black stripes on sides. No stripes on the face. Short round ears. White-to-yellow belly. Long, thin, well-furred tail.

Origin/Age: native; 1-4 years

Compare: Chipmunks (pp. 117-137) are smaller and have stripes on their faces. The White-tailed Antelope Squirrel (pg. 141) lacks dark stripes on its sides. Look for the reddish orange head, neck and shoulders to help identify the Golden-mantled.

Habitat: open woodlands, mountain meadows, forest edges, coniferous forests, elevations above the tree line from 5,000-12,500 feet (1,525-3,810 m)

Home: burrow, up to 25' (7.6 m) long, several feet deep, no excess dirt at the entrance, burrow system has many side tunnels and chambers and several entrances, main entrance is under logs or rocks, chambers lined with leaves, dried grass and bark

Food: omnivore; green plants, seeds, insects, carrion, small lizards, nesting birds

Sounds: variety of sharp chirps, squeals when frightened, growls when confronted

Breeding: Apr-May mating; 28-30 days gestation

Young: 2-8 offspring once per year from May to June; born naked with eyes closed, independent after weaning, aboveground by about 8-10 weeks

Signs: small round entrance holes under logs or rocks, worn path to and from the burrow; scat is rarely seen

Activity: diurnal; most active in early morning and again in late afternoon, but can be seen during the middle of the day, usually seen running quickly back and forth to the burrow, becomes much less active during long hot spells

Tracks: hind paw 1½" (4 cm) long with 5 toes, forepaw ¾" (2 cm) long with 4 toes; tracks usually seen around burrow entrance in dry sandy soils and dirt

Stan's Notes: The reddish orange head, neck and shoulders of the Golden-mantled give this species its common name "mantled," referring to the top part of the animal. A common and widespread ground squirrel in western states, but in Arizona it occurs only in east central and northern locations at elevations between 5,000-12,500 feet (1,525-3,810 m). A solitary squirrel that can be rather bold. Known to beg for handouts at campgrounds and picnic areas and easily observed in many places and habitats.

Frequently seen with other species such as chipmunks and pikas. Often mistaken for a chipmunk due to its dark and light stripes, but lacks any striping on its face or head. Takes dust baths to help maintain its thick fur, rolling in fine grain or dry dirt.

Feeds on a variety of foods and uses its large cheek pouches to carry food back to its burrow for storage and consumption later. Each fall it puts on an extra layer of fat in preparation for winter hibernation. Males, which are slightly larger than females, add more fat at this time. During hibernation it will occasionally wake to feed on its stored food cache. Arouses every 5-7 days during hibernation, but may stay inactive for up to 14 days during the coldest, darkest part of winter. Hibernates from October to April in most parts of its range in Arizona.

Rock Squirrel
Spermophilus variegatus

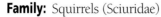

Family: Squirrels (Sciuridae)

Size: L 11-13" (28-33 cm); T 6-8" (15-20 cm)

Weight: 1-2 lb. (.5-.9 kg)

Description: Long, narrow brown (sometimes brown-to-rust) body mottled with gray to tan. White ring around the eyes. Short round ears. Short legs. Long, thick bushy tail.

Origin/Age: native; 1-5 years

Compare: Arizona Gray Squirrel (pg. 177) lacks a mottled appearance and lives in only scattered locations in the state. The Mexican Fox Squirrel (pg. 181) is larger, has a larger, bushier tail and is limited in range to the far southeastern tip of Arizona.

Habitat: rocky fields and hillsides, canyons, talus fields, shrublands, elevations below 8,300' (2,530 m)

Home: burrow, up to 20' (6.1 m) long and often only several feet deep, no excess dirt at the entrance, many side tunnels and several entrance and exit holes, chamber lined with leaves, dried grass and especially tree bark stripped from the tree line

Food: omnivore; green plants, seeds, insects, fruit, nuts, bird eggs, baby mice, baby rabbits, carrion

Sounds: usually silent, females give a sharp clear whistle followed by a low-pitched trill when threatened or alarmed

Breeding: usually April mating; 27-28 days gestation

Young: 3-9 offspring once per year in April; born naked with eyes closed, becomes independent after it is weaned, seen aboveground by about 8-10 weeks

165

Signs: small round entrance holes under large rocks, worn path to and from the burrow; scat is rarely seen since the animal often defecates in its burrow or in dense vegetation

Activity: diurnal; most active in early morning and again in late afternoon, can be seen during the middle of the day, sometimes seen sunning itself on large rocks, will become much less active during long hot spells, also becomes inactive during the colder parts of winter

Tracks: hind paw 2¼" (5.5 cm) long with 5 toes, forepaw 1½" (4 cm) long with 4 toes; tracks often seen near burrow entrance

Stan's Notes: A squirrel of rocky hillsides, canyons, talus fields and dense vegetation below 8,300 feet (2,530 m). Can also be seen in shrublands and juniper woodlands in higher elevations. Increasingly found in urban and suburban areas that have large rocks or retaining walls. Occurs throughout most of Arizona and is expanding its range in many places outside the state.

An expert climber, often climbing trees and bushes to find nuts and fruit. Often confused with Arizona Gray Squirrel (pg. 177) when it is in trees. An opportunistic feeder, foraging on whatever is ripe or available at the time. Fills its large internal cheek pouches to help transport excess food back to the burrow for consumption. During the growing season, it prefers green plants and flowers. Also eats carrion, insects and other protein when available. Has been known to catch, kill and eat baby rabbits, nesting birds or bird eggs.

Apparently does not store food in its burrow like other ground squirrels. Instead, it relies on accumulated fat for survival during bad weather. In colder parts of its range, it hibernates for short durations. Remains active all year in warmer parts of its range.

Usually colonial, with dominant males defending larger areas of territory during breeding season. Dominant females push out less dominant females and also subordinate males so they can be closer to dominant males during breeding season. Rock Squirrel densities are low, with only 5-6 individuals per acre. During the non-breeding season, adults occupy individual home ranges.

Only moderately social; adults don't interact with others outside of breeding season. Individuals familiar with each other approach one another head on and touch noses. Unfamiliar squirrels will approach each other at right angles with many threat displays.

Red Squirrel
Tamiasciurus hudsonicus

Family: Squirrels (Sciuridae)

Size: L 7-9" (18-23 cm); T 4-7" (10-18 cm)

Weight: 5-9 oz. (142-255 g)

Description: Overall rusty red, with brighter red fur on sides. Bright white belly. Distinctive white ring around eyes. Large, fluffy red tail with a black tip. Black line separating the red back from the white belly in summer. Tufted ears in winter.

Origin/Age: native; 2-5 years

Compare: Abert's Squirrel (pg. 173) occurs in color morphs other than red and has large ear tufts. Mexican Fox Squirrel (pg. 181) has an extremely limited range. Range maps will help identify this species.

Habitat: forests, suburban and urban yards, parks, elevations from 6,000-12,000' (1,830-3,660 m)

Home: nest (drey) made mainly with grapevine bark and dried leaves, in a tree cavity or burrow, may build a ball-shaped nest or take an Abert's Squirrel nest

Food: omnivore; pine cone seeds and other seeds, nuts, fruit, acorns, corn, mushrooms; also eats baby birds, bird eggs and carrion

Sounds: loud raspy chatters or wheezy barks when upset or threatened, may bark nonstop for up to an hour, distinctive buzz-like calls given by the male when chasing a female to mate

Breeding: Mar-Apr mating; 33-35 days gestation

Young: 2-5 offspring once per year from April to May; born naked with eyes closed, weaned and on its own after 7-8 weeks

drying mushrooms

scat

Signs: discarded pine cone parts (midden) in a pile on the ground under a tree branch, acorns and other large nuts with a single ragged hole at one end and nutmeat missing

Activity: diurnal; active year-round, but may hole up for a couple days in the nest during very cold, hot or rainy weather

Tracks: hind paw 1½" (4 cm) long with 5 toes, forepaw ¾" (2 cm) long with 4 toes; 1 set of 4 tracks; forepaws fall side by side and behind hind prints

Stan's Notes: This species is also called Chickaree or Pine Squirrel. Although small in size, Red Squirrel has a big attitude and is well known for chasing away larger Abert's Squirrels and other small mammals. However, the success of the Red Squirrel is a function of food resources, not feistiness.

Usually associated with pine trees, but can be in non-coniferous habitats. Feeds heavily on pine cone seeds. Cuts the cones from trees and carries them to a specific spot to eat. A large pile of discarded cone parts, known as a midden, accumulates under the perch. Caches up to a bushel of fresh cones in the midden to eat later. Large middens are usually the result of several squirrels using the same favorite perch over time, with one taking over the spot when another dies. Consumes Amanita mushrooms, which are poisonous to people, without ill effects. Hangs mushrooms to dry on tree branches for future consumption.

Like the Abert's Squirrel, it constructs leaf nests (dreys), but does not build as many. Sometimes will build its nest in a burrow. May construct a small ball-shaped nest from lichen and grass.

Several males will chase a female on tree branches prior to mating. A male may mate with more than one female, but the female is receptive to mating only once on one day in late winter or spring.

The most seasonally dimorphic of squirrels, molting in late spring and again in early autumn. Black morph and white albinos occur but are quite uncommon, unlike other squirrel species.

The genus *Tamiasciurus* is only in North America and includes one other species, Douglas Squirrel (not shown), which occurs in the Pacific Northwest. The species name *hudsonicus* was given because the Red Squirrel ranges as far north in Canada to Hudson Bay and west across Canada and most of Alaska. In fact, it has one of the widest distributions of any squirrel in North America.

gray morph

Abert's Squirrel
Sciurus aberti

Family: Squirrels (Sciuridae)

Size: L 9-11" (23-28 cm); T 8-10" (20-25 cm)

Weight: 1¼-1¾ lb. (.6-1.7 kg)

Description: A wide variety of colors from gray to reddish to brown and black. Gray morph has a white chest and belly, occasionally with a white tail. Brown morph is all brown. Black morph is entirely black. Long "tasseled" ear tufts during winter. Very fluffy large tail.

Origin/Age: native; 2-5 years

Compare: Red Squirrel (pg. 169) is smaller, has a smaller tail and lacks the ear tufts. Arizona Gray Squirrel (pg. 177) is larger and lacks ear tufts.

Habitat: Ponderosa Pine forests, open coniferous mountain forests, elevations above 6,000' (1,830 m)

Home: nest (drey) constructed with small sticks up to 24" (61 cm) wide, occasionally built in the midst of mistletoe infestation, chamber lined with grasses and other soft plant material, most are at least 20' (6.1 m) from the ground on the south side of a Ponderosa Pine tree, near the trunk

Food: omnivore; Ponderosa Pine tree seeds, inner bark, buds and flowers, fungi, berries, carrion

Sounds: threat calls, alarm barks, teeth chattering, screams

Breeding: Mar-Apr mating; 44-46 days gestation

Young: 2-4 offspring once per year; born with eyes closed, eyes open at about 30 days, well developed at 6 weeks, may leave mother at 9-10 weeks, remains with family several more weeks

black morph

brown morph

Kaibab

Signs: small debris pile of pine cone parts, small twigs without needles or outer bark laying about on the ground

Activity: diurnal; active all day year-round, usually begins feeding late in the morning, several hours after sunrise

Tracks: hind paw 2¾-3" (7-7.5 cm) long with 5 toes, forepaw 1½" (4 cm) long with 4 toes; 1 set of 4 tracks; forepaws fall side by side and behind hind prints

Stan's Notes: Also known as Tassel-eared Squirrel due to the long hairs on its ears during winter. Occurs in isolated mountainous pockets in Arizona, Colorado, Utah and New Mexico. Almost always associated with Ponderosa Pine forests, being dependent on several parts of the tree for food.

A well-studied species in Arizona, known to feed in winter on the inner bark (phloem) of particular trees such as the Ponderosa Pine. Trees that are edible in winter are chemically and physiologically different from other trees in the forest, having less toxic chemicals such as monoterpenes. These trees represent less than 10 percent of all trees in a given area.

Feeds mainly on seeds during the rest of the year. It is estimated that while the Abert's eats up to 75 percent of all Ponderosa Pine seeds in a forest, there are still enough seeds left to reproduce more trees.

Uses its nest year-round, retreating there every night. Spends up to several successive days in the nest during harsh winter weather. Will store seeds on the ground, but not in the nest.

Flicks its large tail to communicate with the other squirrels, along with foot stomping. During courtship, males follow females up and down trees. These chases can go on for hours and result in copulation several times a day.

Not common in Arizona in the early 1900s, but its numbers have increased after restrictions were placed on hunting. Not especially territorial and mostly solitary except during the breeding season. Males have larger home ranges than females. Population trends to more males than females.

A unique variety called the Kaibab Squirrel occurs north of the Grand Canyon. It has dark gray fur wih a deep reddish stripe on its back and a pure white tail.

Arizona Gray Squirrel
Sciurus arizonensis

Family: Squirrels (Sciuridae)

Size: L 12-14" (30-36 cm); T 8-9" (20-23 cm)

Weight: 1½-2¼ lb. (.7-1 kg)

Description: Overall gray with a red-to-brown tinge on back. White chest and belly and white ring around the eyes. Small round ears. Large, bushy gray tail with silver-tipped hairs. May have a dark tail, nearly black, with a white underside or white edges.

Origin/Age: native; 2-5 years

Compare: Smaller than the Mexican Fox Squirrel (pg. 181), which is rusty orange and is found in the far southeastern corner of Arizona. Abert's Squirrel (pg. 173) is smaller and has large ear tufts. Rock Squirrel (pg. 165) is similar in size, but it has a mottled appearance and does not live in trees.

Habitat: woodlands, elevations from 5,000-7,000' (1,525-2,135 m)

Home: leaf nest (drey) in summer, up to 24" (61 cm) wide, lined with soft plant material, usually with a side entrance, in tree branches, during winter nest is in a tree cavity, also used for birthing; may build and use up to 6 nests in its territory

Food: omnivore; nuts, acorns, seeds, fruit, mushrooms, bird eggs, baby birds, mice, insects, carrion

Sounds: usually silent; chucking calls or barking alarms

Breeding: spring (Apr-May) mating; 50-60 days gestation

Young: 2-4 offspring once per year; born naked with eyes closed, eyes open at about 30 days, leaves mother and is on its own at about 3 months

Signs: large leaf nests in trees, often seen feeding on the ground

Activity: diurnal; active year-round, usually begins feeding early in the morning, taking a break at midday, then active again in late afternoon, not seen as much when there are young in the nest

Tracks: hind paw 2-2¼" (5-5.5 cm) long with 5 toes, forepaw 1" (2.5 cm) long with 4 toes; 1 set of 4 tracks; forepaws fall side by side and behind hind prints

Stan's Notes: Not a very common species in Arizona, found in limited parts of central and southern Arizona in mid-elevations. Usually in canyons with abundant walnuts and acorns and not far from a water source such as a stream. Usually seen feeding on the ground, looking for fallen nuts and pine cone seeds.

When in trees it is usually heading to or from the nest. Will freeze either on the ground or in a tree when it senses danger. Gives a bark warning call when it sees predators.

Secretive, but where it comes in contact with people it becomes accustomed and will readily come to bird feeders for spilled seed. Very similar to the Eastern Gray Squirrel (not shown), which does not occur in Arizona.

Breeding often starts when flowers bloom in spring. Presumably the squirrel consumes the flowers, which are high in vitamin A and stimulate the reproductive cycle. Males chase the females for extended periods of time and engage in a short wrestling match before they mate. Not all females will breed in the same year.

This tree squirrel has suffered major habitat loss in Mexico due to logging and forest clearing for various agricultural uses and is now considered a threatened species there. The same could be true for it in the future in Arizona because populations here are small, making it vulnerable to loss of habitat.

Mexican Fox Squirrel
Sciurus nayaritensis

Family: Squirrels (Sciuridae)

Size: L 14-16" (36-40 cm); T 8-12" (20-30 cm)

Weight: 1½-2½ lb. (.7-1.1 kg)

Description: Gray with yellow and orange highlights. Bright rusty orange chin, chest, belly and legs. Large and fluffy rust tail, may be dark with a white edge or orange or gray. Female slightly larger than male.

Origin/Age: native; 2-5 years

Compare: Red Squirrel (pg. 169) is half the size and lacks a large tail. Abert's Squirrel (pg. 173) is smaller and has large ear tufts. Rock Squirrel (pg. 165) is gray, has a smaller tail and lives mainly on the ground. This is the only large tree squirrel in Arizona's Chiricahua Mountains. Range will help identify.

Habitat: woodlands, from 5,000-8,500' (1,525-2,590 m)

Home: leaf nest (drey) in summer, up to 24" (61 cm) wide, lined with soft plant material, usually with a side entrance, in a major fork near the main trunk of a tree, in winter nest is in a tree cavity and occupied by several individuals if enough food is available, also used for birthing; may build and use up to 6 nests

Food: omnivore; nuts, corn, seeds, fruit, mushrooms, bird eggs, baby birds, mice, insects, carrion

Sounds: usually silent; barking and chucking alarm calls

Breeding: spring mating; 40-45 days gestation

Young: 2-4 offspring once per year; born with eyes closed, eyes open at about 30 days, leaves mother and is on its own at about 3 months

Signs: large leaf nests in trees, often seen feeding on the ground

Activity: diurnal; active year-round, usually begins feeding early in the morning, taking a break at midday, then active again late in the afternoon

Tracks: hind paw 2¾-3" (7-7.5 cm) long with 5 toes, forepaw 1½" (4 cm) long with 4 toes; 1 set of 4 tracks; forepaws fall side by side and behind hind prints

Stan's Notes: The common name for this squirrel, "Mexican," is because it occurs mainly in Mexico. Found in the mountains of Mexico with just a thin, finger-like range extending into a very small portion of southeastern Arizona. This is the largest squirrel within its range and is the only tree squirrel in the Chiricahua Mountains living in the pine-oak forests of canyons.

Also known as Chiricahua Mountain Squirrel, Apache Squirrel and Nayarit Squirrel. Very similar to the Eastern Fox Squirrel (not shown), which was once considered the same species, but is not found in Arizona.

A secretive squirrel that spends much of its time on the ground. Leaves the nest early in the morning and often does not return until the end of the day except on hot days, when it will return at midday for a short break. Active all year.

Spends more time farther away from trees, searching for food on the ground and traveling. Instead of quickly running up a tree to escape danger, it often freezes and tries to blend in. Reported to be clumsy in trees, sometimes falling out of a tree or slipping on the trunk.

One of the only squirrels that apparently does not cache food for later consumption. Because of this it spends less time gathering and storing food than other squirrels, and more time looking for seeds, nuts and other items to eat each day all year.

Gunnison's Prairie Dog
Cynomys gunnisoni

Family: Squirrels (Sciuridae)

Size: L 10-12½" (25-32 cm); T 2-2½" (5-6 cm)

Weight: 1-2½ lb. (.5-1.1 kg)

Description: Overall yellowish tan to cinnamon with tiny black flecks. Lighter undersides. Top of head and area just above eyes are darker than the rest of body. Small round ears that do not stand upright. Short thin tail, one-third of it white from the tip.

Origin/Age: native; 1-5 years

Compare: Black-tailed Prairie Dog (pg. 189) is very similar, but has a black-tipped tail. Gunnison's does not occur in the former range of the Black-tailed, so use range to help identify.

Habitat: grasslands, mountain valleys, elevations between 6,000-12,000' (1,830-3,660 m)

Home: extensive burrow system, up to 30' (9.1 m) long and up to 5' (1.5 m) deep, small mounds or no dirt at entrance, many side tunnels and chambers and several entrances, intertwines with neighbor burrows, dried grass lines nest chamber

Food: herbivore; grasses, sedges, roots

Sounds: variety of calls, high-pitched bark or alarm call

Breeding: Mar-Apr mating; 30-33 days gestation

Young: 3-8 offspring once per year; born naked with eyes closed, seen aboveground by about 4-7 weeks in June and July

Signs: several mounds of dome-shaped dirt with a single entrance hole, many burrows do not have dirt mounds

Activity: diurnal; active all day, remains underground on cold and rainy days, becomes inactive during the middle of the day in hot weather, can be seen during winter in lower elevations when weather permits

Tracks: hind paw 2-2½" (5-6 cm) long with 5 toes, forepaw 1" (2.5 cm) long with 4 toes; tracks usually seen around burrow entrance in dry sandy soils and dirt

Stan's Notes: Found in northeastern and north central Arizona, occurring in high elevations in loose aggregates of families or clans, called colonies. Colonies are sometimes found in residential areas, especially with the expansion of human development.

Like other prairie dogs, the Gunnison's does not require any free-standing water. Instead, all of its water needs are met through the green plants and roots it eats. About 60 percent of its time above-ground is spent gathering food and feeding. It gathers grasses in large amounts, storing the material in underground chambers for consumption later or for lining a nesting chamber.

Adults start to enter hibernation by October and emerge by mid-April. Hibernation may last 4-6 months, with shorter hibernation times occurring at lower elevations.

According to results of a study, the call of the Gunnison's appears to convey specific information about the number and type of predators approaching. This allows others in the colony to react appropriately such as looking up for an avian predator or around for a terrestrial predator.

All species of prairie dogs in the United States were considered a nuisance in the past and shot, poisoned or trapped. Despite years of persecution, they have have managed to make a comeback and now have stable populations in many areas. With the successful reintroduction of the Black-footed Ferret (pg. 223), whose main diet is prairie dogs, all prairie dog populations may once again be brought back into balance.

Black-tailed Prairie Dog
Cynomys ludovicianus

XTIRPATED
no longer found

FORMER
RANGE

Family: Squirrels (Sciuridae)

Size: L 12-14" (30-36 cm); T 3-4½" (7.5-11 cm)

Weight: 1½-3 lb. (.7-1.4 kg)

Description: Uniform tan to light brown (sometimes cinnamon) with cream-to-white undersides. Short round ears that do not stand upright. Short, thin black-tipped tail, covered with short hairs.

Origin/Age: native; 1-4 years

Compare: There are no known populations of Black-tailed Prairie Dog presently in the state, but the species does occur in New Mexico and Colorado, making it possible for it to reenter Arizona at any time.

Habitat: grasslands, fields, pastures, elevations up to 6,000' (1,830 m)

Home: extensive burrow systems, up to 30' (9.1 m) long and up to 7' (2.1 m) deep, large mounds of excess dirt at entrance, many side tunnels and chambers, several entrances, some burrows are intertwined with neighbor burrows, dried grass lines the nest chamber

Food: herbivore; grasses, sedges, roots

Sounds: variety of calls, high-pitched bark or alarm call given by several individuals, one after another

Breeding: Feb-Mar mating; 30-35 days gestation

Young: 4-8 offspring once per year; born naked with eyes closed, goes aboveground by about 4-7 weeks in May and June

den entrance

barking

Signs: many large volcano-shaped domes with a single entrance hole, cut grass around the vicinity of the entrance

Activity: diurnal; active all day year-round, remains underground on extremely cold or rainy days, becomes inactive during the middle of the day in hot weather, becomes less active in winter

Tracks: hind paw 2-2½" (5-6 cm) long with 5 toes, forepaw 1" (2.5 cm) long with 4 toes; tracks usually seen around burrow entrance in dry sandy soils and dirt

Stan's Notes: This species was once found in large numbers in the southeastern corner of the state. It was poisoned and trapped in Arizona in the early 1900s, when land was being cleared for cattle grazing. By the 1930s it was completely removed (extirpated) and is thought not to occur in the state now. A similar species, the Gunnison's Prairie Dog (pg. 185), is found in Arizona, but not in the historic range of the Black-tailed. Any prairie dog seen outside the range of the Gunnison's needs to be documented and reported to the Arizona Game and Fish Department.

Makes its home in open fields and grassy pastures. Lives in groups, creating towns that can be large and expansive, with hundreds of mounded entrance holes dotting the landscape.

Active during the day, spending most of its time aboveground, feeding on green plants. Does not hibernate, but will stay underground for several days during inclement weather.

A prairie dog has cones in its eyes, but no rods. As a result, it does not see very well in dim light or while underground.

Reproduces only once each year, with just 30 percent of young females reproducing in their first year. Young are born naked and eyes stay closed for 5 weeks. They are fully furred by 3 weeks and fully grown by autumn. Goes aboveground in late May and June.

At first, the young don't wander far from their burrow. Gradually, as they grow, they start to explore farther away in fields. Activities include playing, chasing, play fighting, wrestling and running up to parents. Adults rarely exhibit these behaviors.

Adults mutually groom one another or touch noses, sniffing each other. An individual will stand erect at the entrance to its burrow and give a loud sharp bark at any sign of danger, throwing its head back while standing on hind legs. The bark is usually followed by other colony members echoing the call.

Botta's Pocket Gopher

Thomomys bottae

Family: Pocket Gophers (Geomyidae)

Size: L 5-7" (13-18 cm); T 2-3½" (5-9 cm)

Weight: 5-7 oz. (142-198 g)

Description: Highly variable in color from light brown and tan or yellow to dark brown to nearly black. Very small ears, but visible, with a black patch behind each ear. Small eyes. Short legs, pink feet and extremely long claws on front paws. Short naked tail. Size is highly variable and male is larger than the female.

Origin/Age: native; 2-5 years

Compare: Southern Pocket Gopher (pg. 197) and Northern Pocket Gopher (pg. 197) are similar to Botta's, but they are extremely limited in range in the state. Look for the large front claws and short legs to help identify the gophers.

Habitat: loose sandy soils, fields, meadows, pastures, golf courses, cemeteries, roadside ditches, elevations below 5,000' (1,525 m)

Home: network of tunnels, usually with 2 levels, some about 6" (15 cm) deep, used for gathering food, deeper tunnels down to 6' (1.8 m) are used for nesting and raising young

Food: herbivore; roots, bulbs, rhizomes

Sounds: inconsequential; rarely, if ever, heard

Breeding: spring mating; 50-55 days gestation

Young: 2-6 offspring once per year; born naked and helpless with eyes closed

193

Signs: mounds of excess dirt as wide as 24" (61 cm) resulting from tunneling, ridges of dirt pushed up from tunneling; opening to tunnel system only rarely seen (would require digging into a dirt mound)

Activity: diurnal, nocturnal; active year-round, alternates several hours of activity with several hours of sleep

Tracks: forepaw ⅞" (2.3 cm) long, hind paw slightly smaller, both with well-defined claw marks; spends almost all of its time in its underground tunnel system, so tracks are rarely seen

Stan's Notes: There are 35 gopher species, all unique to North America. Botta's Pocket Gopher is found from Texas to California, south into Mexico and north to Colorado, Nevada and Oregon. It occurs throughout Arizona and can be very common in places.

Specialized fur-lined cheek pouches or "pockets" give the pocket gopher its common name. Able to stuff large amounts of food or nesting material in its pouches, which extend from its cheeks to front shoulders. Cleans the pouches by turning them inside out.

Digs with its powerful front legs and long sharp claws, preferring loose sandy soils. Specialized lips close behind its large incisor teeth, keeping dirt out of the mouth while it digs. Incisor teeth are coated with enamel and grow throughout its life. Must gnaw on hard objects to keep its teeth sharp and prevent them from growing too large and rendering them useless. Sensitive hairs and bristles (vibrissae) on the wrists and tip of tail help it feel its way through tunnels. A narrow pelvis enables it to turn around while in tunnels. Its fur can lay forward or backward and allows the animal to back up without slowing down. Has a good sense of smell, but poor hearing and eyesight.

Lives entirely underground. Feeds on roots and bulbs of different plant species, depending upon the season and availability, and stores some food in underground chambers. Has been known to pull entire plants underground by the roots. Solitary except to mate, with only one animal living in a set of tunnels and mounds.

Has adapted well to human activity, often taking up residence in open grassy yards. This animal is very beneficial to the land since its digging aerates the soil, which allows for better drainage and nutrient mixing. However, it can be destructive to gardens and fields because it eats many of the plants.

Similar species on next page

The word "gopher" is frequently used to describe a wide range of burrowing rodents that includes chipmunks and ground squirrels, but the term is properly restricted to pocket gophers, all of which have fur-lined cheek pouches on both sides of the mouth.

Pocket gophers can be difficult to distinguish, as they all share similar characteristics in size, shape and color. Many are separated only by chromosomal and biochemical differences, so consider the range when attempting to identify a gopher. While the Botta's Pocket Gopher is found throughout Arizona, the range of the Southern Pocket Gopher is restricted to just a small region on the border in southeastern Arizona. The range of Northern Pocket Gopher is similarly limited to a small area on the northwestern border of the state.

Southern Pocket Gopher 6-9"

Northern Pocket Gopher 7-10"

Mountain Cottontail
Sylvilagus nuttallii

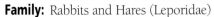

Family: Rabbits and Hares (Leporidae)

Size: L 11½-12½" (29-32 cm); T 1-2" (2.5-5 cm)

Weight: 1½-2½ lb. (.7-1.1 kg)

Description: Overall gray to light brown with the center back darker than the sides. Black-tipped hairs give a salt-and-pepper appearance. White underside. Large pointed ears, the width of head, slightly furred, with a black outside edge. Rusty red nape. Brown tail with a white cotton-like underside.

Origin/Age: native; 1-3 years

Compare: Cottontails are so similar, use their ranges to help identify. The Desert Cottontail (pg. 203) occurs in Arizona below 6,500' (1,980 m). The Eastern Cottontail (pg. 207) is mainly in southeastern and central Arizona below 6,500' (1,980 m).

Habitat: mountain valleys, coniferous subalpine forests, rock piles, shrublands, thickets, elevations from 6,000-11,000' (1,830-3,355 m)

Home: shallow nest, lined with soft plant material and fur, covered with dry grasses and leaves

Food: herbivore; grass and other green plants in spring and summer; sage, saplings, twigs, bark and other woody plants in winter

Sounds: loud high-pitched scream or squeal when caught by a predator such as a fox or coyote

Breeding: late Feb-Jul mating; 28-30 days gestation; starts to breed at 8 months

Young: 3-6 offspring 3-4 times per year; born naked and helpless with eyes closed

199

Signs: small woody twigs and branches near the ground are cleanly cut off and at an angle, while browse from deer and elk is higher up and has a ragged edge (due to lack of upper incisors in deer and elk), bark is stripped off saplings and shrubs at the level of snow; pea-sized, round, dry, woody, light brown pellets

Activity: nocturnal, crepuscular; active year-round, often active during midday, stays in burrow for several days during inclement weather in winter

Tracks: hind paw 3-4" (7.5-10 cm) long, forepaw 1" (2.5 cm) long, small and round; 1 set of 4 tracks; forepaws fall one in front of the other behind hind prints

Stan's Notes: A rabbit species of areas above 6,000 feet (1,830 m), occurring in northeastern and central eastern Arizona. Tends to stay away from densely vegetated areas and wetlands.

Common name comes from the mountainous habitat where it is found and its cotton ball-like tail. Given the species name *nuttallii* and also called Nuttall's Cottontail after the early naturalist, Thomas Nuttall (1786-1859).

Active all year. Tends to be more active during the day than the other cottontail species. Often seen feeding during the middle of the day. Uses the burrows of other animals in winter, where it will hole up for a few days during bad weather. Cools itself on hot summer days, stretching out in shady areas.

Can run up to 15 mph (24 km/h) for short distances, which enables it to evade some predators. Makes a short dash when alarmed, stops and crouches, often facing away from the danger. Uses a set of well-worn trails during winter, usually under a thick cover of bushes.

Doesn't interbreed with the Desert Cottontail (pg. 203) or Eastern Cottontail (pg. 207) even where habitats overlap. Stops breeding in extreme drought conditions, reducing the competition for food and the nutritional requirements for females that otherwise would have been nursing.

Mothers nurse their babies at dawn and dusk, but may stay away for up to 24 hours at a time. Once the young open their eyes and are moving around outside the nest, they are on their own and get no further help from their mother.

Desert Cottontail
Sylvilagus audubonii

Family: Rabbits and Hares (Leporidae)

Size: L 12-13½" (30-34.5 cm); T 1-2" (2.5-5 cm)

Weight: 1¾-3 lb. (.8-1.4 kg)

Description: Overall gray to light brown with the center of the back darker than the sides. Longer black-tipped hairs, giving a grizzled appearance. Large hairless ears, longer than the length of head, with a black outside edge. Distinctive rusty red nape. Brown tail with a white cotton-like underside.

Origin/Age: native; 1-3 years

Compare: Since cottontails are so similar, use range to help identify. The Mountain Cottontail (pg. 199) is in northeastern and central eastern Arizona above 6,000' (1,830 m). Eastern Cottontail (pg. 207) is in central Arizona below 6,500' (1,980 m).

Habitat: wide variety such as open fields, golf courses, brush or rock piles, along streams, shrublands, semideserts, deserts, below 6,500' (1,980 m)

Home: shallow nest, lined with soft plant material and fur, covered with dry grasses and leaves

Food: herbivore; grass, dandelions, other green plants in spring and summer; twigs, bark and other woody plants in winter

Sounds: loud high-pitched scream or squeal when caught by a predator such as a fox or coyote

Breeding: year-round mating; 28 days gestation; starts to breed at 3 months

Young: 3-6 offspring 3-5 times per year; born naked and helpless with eyes closed

Signs: small woody twigs and branches near the ground are cleanly cut off and at an angle, while browse from deer and elk is higher up and has a ragged edge (due to lack of upper incisors in deer and elk); pea-sized, round, dry, woody, light brown pellets

scat

Activity: nocturnal, crepuscular; often very active during late winter and early spring when males fight to breed with females

Tracks: hind paw 3-4" (7.5-10 cm) long, forepaw 1" (2.5 cm) long, small and round; 1 set of 4 tracks; forepaws fall one in front of the other behind hind prints

Stan's Notes: The most widespread of western cottontail species from Montana to Texas and California. Found in elevations below 6,500 feet (1,980 m) throughout Arizona; not seen in the central eastern mountains. Common name comes from the semidesert-like habitat where it is found and its cotton ball-like tail.

Usually freezes, hunkers down and flattens ears if danger is near. Able to leap up to 12-15 feet (3.7-4.5 m) in a single bound while running, jumping sideways while running to break its scent trail. Can run as fast as 15 mph (24 km/h) for a short distance, which enables it to elude some predators. Uses a well-worn set of trails in winter, usually under thick cover of bushes. When flushed, it runs quickly in a zigzag pattern, circling back to its starting spot. On hot, lazy summer days, it will stretch out in shady areas to cool itself.

Males often remain in a small area of only 10-15 acres (4-6 ha), while females reside in areas about half that size. Usually not a territorial animal, but fights will break out among males during mating season. Interspersed with chasing, males face each other, kick with front feet and jump high into the air.

After mating, the female excavates a small area for a nest, lines it with soft plants and fur from her chest for comfort and camouflages the entrance. Mothers nurse their babies at dawn and dusk, but may stay away for up to a day at a time. Once the young open their eyes and are moving around outside the nest, they are on their own and no longer receive help from their mother.

A successful rabbit species, with females usually breeding before they reach 1 year of age and some producing up to 35 offspring annually. Most of the cottontail young, however, do not live any longer than a year.

Eastern Cottontail
Sylvilagus floridanus

Family: Rabbits and Hares (Leporidae)

Size: L 14-18" (36-45 cm); T 1-2" (2.5-5 cm)

Weight: 2-4 lb. (.9-1.8 kg)

Description: Overall gray to light brown. Black-tipped hairs give it a grizzled appearance. Usually has a small white (rarely black) spot on forehead between the ears. Large pointed ears, rarely with a black outside edge. Distinctive rusty red nape. Brown tail with a white cotton-like underside.

Origin/Age: native; 1-3 years

Compare: Since cottontails are so similar, use range to help identify. Desert Cottontail (pg. 203) is smaller and much more widespread in Arizona. Mountain Cottontail (pg. 199) occurs in the northeastern corner of the state above 6,000' (1,830 m).

Habitat: wide variety such as open fields, brush piles, rock piles, along rivers and streams, woodlands, thickets, elevations below 6,500' (1,980 m)

Home: shallow nest, lined with soft plant material and fur, covered with dry grasses and leaves

Food: herbivore; grass, dandelions, other green plants in spring and summer; saplings, twigs, bark and other woody plants in winter

Sounds: loud high-pitched scream or squeal when caught by a predator such as a fox or coyote

Breeding: late Feb-Mar mating; 30 days gestation; starts to breed at 3 months

Young: 3-6 offspring up to 5 times per year; born naked and helpless with eyes closed

camouflaged

scat

Signs: small woody twigs and branches near the ground are cleanly cut off and at an angle, while browse from deer is higher up and has a ragged edge (due to the lack of upper incisors in deer), bark is stripped off of saplings and shrubs; dry, pea-sized light brown pellets, round and woody; soft green pellets are ingested and rarely seen

Activity: nocturnal, crepuscular; often very active during late winter and early spring when males fight to breed with females

Tracks: hind paw 3-4" (7.5-10 cm) long, forepaw 1" (2.5 cm) long, small and round; 1 set of 4 tracks; forepaws fall one in front of the other behind hind prints

Stan's Notes: The most widespread of the eight cottontail species in North America, seen in the eastern United States and most of Mexico, but found only in southeastern Arizona, extending into central Arizona. Transplanted to many areas that historically did not have cottontails. Common name is for its cotton ball-like tail.

Usually stays in a small area of only a couple acres. Often freezes, hunkers down and flattens ears if danger is near. Quickly runs in a zigzag pattern, circling back to its starting spot when flushed. Able to leap up to 12-15 feet (3.7-4.5 m) in a single bound while running. Also jumps sideways while running to break its scent trail. Uses a set of well-worn trails in winter, usually in thick cover of bushes. Cools itself on hot summer days by stretching out in shaded grassy areas.

Usually not a territorial animal, with fights among males breaking out only during mating season. Interspersed with chasing, males face each other, kick with front feet and jump high into the air.

After mating, the female excavates a small area for a nest, lines it with soft plants and fur from her chest for comfort and camouflages the entrance. Mothers nurse their babies at dawn and dusk. Once the young open their eyes and are moving outside the nest, they are on their

cooling

own and get no further help from their mother. One of the most reproductively successful rabbit species in North America, with some females producing as many as 35 offspring annually; however, most young do not live longer than 1 year.

Like other rabbits and hares, this species produces fecal pellets that are dry and brown or soft and green. Eats the green pellets to regain the nutrition that wasn't digested initially.

Black-tailed Jackrabbit
Lepus californicus

Family: Rabbits and Hares (Leporidae)

Size: L 18-24" (45-61 cm); T 2-3" (5-7.5 cm)

Weight: 4-8 lb. (1.8-3.6 kg)

Description: Gray to light brown in summer with black-tipped hair, giving it a grizzled appearance. Light white belly. Extremely long, black-tipped ears. Long legs. Large hind feet. Large brown eyes. A large, puffy white tail with black on top and extending onto the rump. All white in winter, sometimes with brown patches. Black-tipped white ears.

Origin/Age: native; 1-5 years

Compare: The Antelope Jackrabbit (pg. 215) is larger and has longer ears, with a very distinct white rump and sides, visible when running.

Habitat: semideserts, scrublands, grasslands, elevations below 7,000' (2,135 m)

Home: shallow nest under sagebrush and other shrubs or beneath logs, lined with dry grasses and hair from the mother, uses a burrow in winter

Food: herbivore; green plants in summer, twigs, bark, leaf buds, dried grasses and berries in winter

Sounds: inconsequential; may give a loud, shrill scream when captured by a large predator

Breeding: Feb-May mating; 30-40 days gestation

Young: 1-11 offspring 4-5 times per year; born fully furred with eyes open and incisor teeth erupted, able to move around within an hour of birth

Signs: trails worn between feeding areas and resting sites; hard, dry, woody, slightly flattened, dark brown pellets, ½" (1 cm) wide, or moist green pellets

Activity: mostly nocturnal, crepuscular; can be seen during cloudy or overcast days

Tracks: hind paw 4-5½" (10-14 cm) long and 2" (5 cm) wide, forepaw 1" (2.5 cm) long, small and round; 1 set of 4 tracks; forepaws are slightly offset side by side or fall one in front of the other behind hind prints

Stan's Notes: The most abundant jackrabbit species across most of the western states including throughout Arizona. Sometimes called Jackass Rabbit, although it is actually a type of hare. Hard to misidentify because it is so large and runs with a seesaw-like rocking from front to hind feet. Black on tail and rump is best seen when it runs. Can leap as far as 20 feet (6.1 m) and run up to 45 mph (72 km/h) for a short distance, slowing to a series of low leaps from 4-10 feet (1.2-3 m).

The enormous ears have a generous blood flow, which dissipates heat during summer. The ears also provide an excellent means of predator detection. The large hind legs facilitate high jumps and quick escapes from predators and are used for defense, kicking and scratching with its claws. Does not like water, but is a good swimmer and may plunge into water to escape a predator.

Usually solitary, but may be seen in large groups, especially in spring when it gathers for mating. Females can be slightly larger than males (bucks), but there are no obvious differences between sexes. When bucks fight, they kick with hind feet and bite.

Rests under logs or other shelter (shade) during the day and will flush only if contact is very close. During winter it snuggles in burrows that may be connected by tunnels, resting with its large ears pressed flat against its back.

Female constructs a simple nest–a shallow depression lined with grasses and fur plucked from her chest. Babies can run within an hour of their birth. They are eating plants at 2 weeks and weaned shortly after, fully independent at 4 weeks. If born early enough in the season, young females can breed before their first winter.

Reingestion of soft fecal pellets (coprophagy) occurs in hares, as it does in rabbits.

Antelope Jackrabbit
Lepus alleni

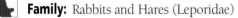

Family: Rabbits and Hares (Leporidae)

Size: L 22-25" (56-64 cm); T 1¾-3" (4.5-7.5 cm)

Weight: 6-9 lb. (2.7-4.1 kg)

Description: Gray to light brown on the sides and back with a light gray-to-white belly. Rump and side hairs raise and flash white during a run or excitement. Very long ears. Big brown eyes. White eye-ring. Long, thin front legs. Large hind feet. Large puffy tail, black on top and white underneath.

Origin/Age: native; 1-5 years

Compare: The Black-tailed Jackrabbit (pg. 211) is smaller, has shorter black-tipped ears and lacks the white flashing sides and rump. Significantly larger than the Desert Cottontail (pg. 203), which has much shorter ears. The limited range of the Antelope Jackrabbit can help to differentiate.

Habitat: deserts, grasslands

Home: shallow nest (form) under logs or shrubs, lined with dry grasses and fur from the mother; does not always make a nest

Food: herbivore; green plants, cactus fruit, leaf buds, dried and fresh grasses, mesquite

Sounds: inconsequential; almost never makes any sound, may give a loud, shrill scream when captured by a large predator

Breeding: year-round mating; 40-45 days gestation

Young: 1-5 offspring 3-4 times per year; born fully furred with eyes open and incisor teeth erupted, able to move around within an hour of birth

flushing

Signs: shallow depressions beneath shrubs and trees; hard, dry, woody, light brown pellets or soft, moist green pellets depending on the food it eats

Activity: mostly nocturnal, crepuscular; can be seen during cloudy or overcast days

Tracks: hind paw 5-6" (13-15 cm) long and 2-2½" (5-6 cm) wide, forepaw 1½" (4 cm) long, small and round; 1 set of 4 tracks; forepaws are slightly offset side by side or fall one in front of the other behind hind prints

Stan's Notes: Closely related to the more common Black-tailed Jackrabbit (pg. 211), which is found throughout Arizona in many different habitats. The largest rabbit-like animal in the state, it is a type of hare. Differs from rabbits in the amount and placement of teeth and in its young, which are born furred and ready to run. Also known as Allen's Hare, Wandering Jackrabbit, Saddle Jack, Mexican Jackrabbit, Burrow Jack and Jackass Rabbit.

Able to leap up to 20 feet (6.1 m) in a single bound and run as fast as 45 mph (72 km/h) for short distances, slowing to a series of low leaps of 4-10 feet (1.2-3 m). Given the common name "Antelope" for its flashing white rump and sides, apparent when it runs due to raised hairs. When the jackrabbit stops to rest, the hairs lay flat and the white disappears, providing camouflage and presumably confusing predators that were following the white.

This species has the largest ears of all jackrabbits. The large ears have a generous blood flow, which dissipates heat in summer. The ears also provide an excellent means of predator detection. Ears are laid back flat against the back when resting. Each ear moves independently to hear both in front and back at the same time.

Usually solitary except for mothers with young. No noticeable differences between sexes. Males (bucks) fight by kicking with the hind feet and biting. Males compete for the females, breeding promiscuously, chasing females until his advances are accepted.

Eats a wide variety of green plants, often standing on hind legs to reach mesquite leaves or feeds on the red fruit of some cacti. Grasses make up about half of the diet, when they can be found. Apparently does not drink from free water sources, but gets all the water it needs from the plants it consumes.

Female builds a simple nest consisting of a shallow depression lined with grasses and fur she has taken from her chest. Babies can run within an hour of birth. The young are eating plants in a couple weeks and weaned and fully independent in a month.

Long-tailed Weasel
Mustela frenata

Family: Weasels and Skunks (Mustelidae)

Size: L 8-16" (20-40 cm); T 3-6" (7.5-15 cm)

Weight: 3-9 oz. (85-255 g)

Description: Light brown in summer with a long black-tipped brown tail, brown feet and white-to-yellow chin, throat, chest and belly. Long tubular body. Short legs. White in the winter with a black-tipped tail. Male slightly larger than female.

Origin/Age: native; 5-10 years

Compare: Much smaller than Black-footed Ferret (pg. 223), which doesn't turn white in winter and is always associated with prairie dogs.

Habitat: forests, fields, grasslands, farms, wet areas, elevations between 6,000-12,000' (1,830-3,660 m)

Home: nest made from grass and fur, usually in an old chipmunk or ground squirrel burrow or underneath logs and rocks; often has several nests in its territory

Food: carnivore, insectivore; small to medium mammals such as mice, voles, chipmunks, squirrels and rabbits; will also eat small birds, bird eggs, carrion and insects

Sounds: single loud trills or rapid trills, squeals

Breeding: summer (Jul-Aug) mating; 30-34 days gestation; ova develop for 8 days after fertilization, then cease development, implantation is delayed up to 8-10 months after mating

Young: 4-8 offspring once per year from April to June

219

Signs: long, thin, often dark scat with a pointed end, contains hair and bones, often on a log or rock, very similar to mink scat

Activity: primarily nocturnal, diurnal mostly during the winter; hunts during the day for several hours, then rests and sleeps for several hours

Tracks: hind paw ¾-1" (2-2.5 cm) long, forepaw slightly smaller, both round with well-defined nail marks, 5 toes on all feet; 1 set of 4 tracks when bounding; 12-20" (30-50 cm) stride

Stan's Notes: This is a very active predator that runs in a series of bounds with its back arched and tail elevated. Found mainly in the mountains up to 12,000 feet (3,660 m).

A good swimmer and will climb trees to pursue squirrels. Quickly locates prey using its excellent eyesight and sense of smell, dashes to grab it, then kills it with several bites to the base of the skull. Favorite foods include mice and voles. Sometimes hunts for larger prey such as rabbits. Eats its fill and caches the rest. Consumes 25-40 percent of its own body weight in food daily.

Uses scents and sounds to communicate with other weasels. Deposits scat on rocks or along trails to mark territory. Male territory covers 25-55 acres (10-22 ha); the female territory is smaller. Both sexes will apply an odoriferous, oily substance secreted from the anal glands on rocks, trees and other prominent landmarks

winter

to communicate their sex, social status, territory and willingness to mate. Can be seen depositing the substance, but the odor is rarely detectible by people, especially after a few days. Will defend territory against other weasels.

Solitary except during mating season and when a mother is with her young. Constructs nest in an abandoned animal burrow or beneath logs and rocks, using grass and the fur of small animals it has eaten for nesting material.

FORMER
RANGE

Black-footed Ferret
Mustela nigripes

Family: Weasels and Skunks (Mustelidae)

Size: L 15½-19" (39-48 cm); T 4-5½" (10-14 cm)

Weight: 1½-2¼ lb. (.7-1 kg)

Description: Body is tan to yellowish brown with a dark stripe down the center of back. Black mask around eyes. Elongated tubular body with short legs. Black legs and feet. Light-colored tail with a black tip.

Origin/Age: native; 5-10 years

Compare: Larger than Long-tailed Weasel (pg. 219), which lacks the black mask, legs and feet of the Ferret.

Habitat: grasslands, fields, prairie dog towns

Home: takes over a prairie dog burrow or ground squirrel tunnel; home range of 20-50 acres (8-20 ha) or more

Food: carnivore; mainly prairie dogs; also eats ground squirrels, rabbits, reptiles and some insects

Sounds: much growling and snarling when cornered

Breeding: winter (Feb-Mar) mating; 42-45 days gestation; no delayed implantation

Young: 3-5 offspring once per year in April or May; first appears aboveground in July, when it is about three-quarters the size of an adult

Signs: narrow piles of freshly excavated dirt at the entrance of a burrow; long, thin, often dark scat with a pointed end, contains hair and bones, very similar to mink scat

Activity: primarily nocturnal, diurnal only during winter when adults are looking for mates and moving from burrow to burrow during the day; most active between one and four o'clock in the morning during the rest of the year, hunts mainly at night until it catches something, then rests for up to 6 days, feeding on its kill

Tracks: hind paw 2-2¾" (5-7 cm) long, forepaw slightly smaller, both round with well-defined nail marks, 5 toes on all feet; 1 set of 4 tracks when bounding; 12-20" (30-50 cm) stride

Stan's Notes: The least known of all weasels in North America. Was listed as an endangered species prior to being declared extinct in 1979, when the last ferret died in a zoo. No wild ferrets were known to exist, but in 1981, a ranch dog in Meeteetse, Wyoming, brought home the body of a Black-footed Ferret, which lead to the discovery of a small wild population. By 1985 the wild population was struck with a fatal disease, killing all but 18 individuals. These few remaining ferrets were trapped and bred in captivity. Starting in 1991 the ferrets were reintroduced back to the wild in several states, including Arizona in 1996.

Black-footed Ferrets have coevolved with prairie dogs and are so closely linked, you can't find ferrets without a prairie dog town. Ferrets use prairie dog burrows for their homes and hunt and eat prairie dogs for food. A ferret might expand the burrow or add chambers and will often leave the burrow and take up residency in another one as it searches for food.

Ferrets live alone in burrows and will come together only during mating or when females have young. Young leave their mothers at the end of their first summer and are sexually mature at 1 year of age. Will start to breed right away and may live up to 10 years in the wild. Extremely nocturnal, only coming aboveground well after dark, and usually back in the burrow well before daylight.

Very susceptible to canine distemper, resulting in many ferret deaths. Also suffers from plague. Highly impacted by poisoning programs designed to control prairie dogs.

Prospects for the survival of the Black-footed Ferret are good as long as the prairie dog population stays healthy and the habitat and prey remain intact.

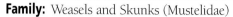

American Badger
Taxidea taxus

Family: Weasels and Skunks (Mustelidae)

Size: L 20-30" (50-76 cm); T 3-6" (7.5-15 cm)

Weight: 8-25 lb. (3.6-11.3 kg)

Description: Coarse, grizzled gray upper and yellowish brown underside. A dark snout with a distinctive white stripe from the nose upward, between the eyes and to the nape. White cheeks and ears. Large wide body. Short powerful legs with long, sharp nonretractable (nonretractile) nails on front feet. Small gray tail. Male larger than female.

Origin/Age: native; 3-10 years

Compare: Look for American Badger's unique body shape, short legs and the white stripe between the eyes.

Habitat: along roads, fields, grasslands, woodland edges, all elevations

Home: large den, often in a road embankment or grassy hillside, digs its own, may overtake and enlarge a prairie dog burrow; uses den for birthing, raising young and during torpor

Food: carnivore, insectivore; small mammals such as voles, mice, chipmunks, rabbits and ground squirrels; also eats small birds, bird eggs, snakes, frogs, toads and insects

Sounds: loud snarls and growls

Breeding: Jul-Aug mating; 30-40 days gestation; implantation delayed until February after mating

Young: 1-5 offspring once per year in March or April; born covered with fine fur and eyes closed, eyes open at about 4 weeks, weaned at about 8 weeks

den entrance

scat

Signs: large pile of unearthed dirt in front of den entrance, can be seen from a great distance, bones, uneaten body parts and scat frequently scattered near the den entrance; long thin scat, segmented, often dark, contains hair and bones

Activity: nocturnal; usually does not leave den until well after dark to hunt for small mammals, occasionally leaves den during the day

Tracks: forepaw and hind paw 2" (5 cm) long and wide, round with narrow pad, separate nail marks, 5 distinct toes on all feet; fore and hind prints fall near each other when walking, 6-12" (15-30 cm) stride

Stan's Notes: The least weasel-like of weasels. Uniquely shaped, its wide flattened body, short powerful legs and narrow snout make it well suited to burrow and live underground. Has second eyelids (nictitating membranes), which protect its eyes while it digs. Uses its long, sharp front claws to dig through coarse rocky soil, expelling dirt between its hind legs like a dog. Can dig fast enough to catch ground squirrels while they are still in their burrows. Has an excellent sense of smell. Believed to be able to determine just by the scent of a burrow whether or not it is occupied.

Secretive and avoids contact with people. Has the reputation of being aggressive, especially a mother defending her young. Very vocal when threatened, snarling and growling loudly.

Hunts cooperatively with coyotes. While a badger excavates one tunnel entrance, a coyote will wait for the occupant to emerge at an auxiliary escape tunnel. Frequently the coyote will chase the occupant back down the burrow to the waiting badger.

It is not a true hibernator, but enters a condition called torpor that resembles hibernation, during which the body temperature falls approximately 10°F (-12°C) and heart rate and respiration decrease to approximately half the normal rate. Torpor lasts only 20-30 hours at a time. Badgers remain awake for up to 24 hours between periods of torpor, during which time body temperature and heart rate return to normal. Because of this energy-saving torpor cycle, the body rarely uses up its stored fat by spring.

Male has a large home range, where several females also may live. Lacks a family structure. Male stays solitary while female raises young on her own. Young stay with the mother until their first autumn, when they are fully grown and can hunt on their own.

RARE

Northern River Otter
Lontra canadensis

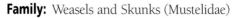

Family: Weasels and Skunks (Mustelidae)

Size: L 2½-3½' (76-107 cm); T 11-20" (28-50 cm)

Weight: 10-30 lb. (4.5-13.5 kg)

Description: Overall dark brown-to-black fur, especially when wet, with a lighter brown-to-gray belly. Silver-to-gray chin and throat. Small ears and eyes. Short snout with white whiskers. Elongated body with a long thick tail, tapered at the tip. Male slightly larger than female.

Origin/Age: native; 7-20 years

Compare: Much larger than the Muskrat (pg. 101), which has a long, thin naked tail. The American Beaver (pg. 105) has a wide flat tail.

Habitat: rivers, streams, medium to large lakes, elevations up to 8,500' (2,590 m)

Home: permanent and temporary dens

Food: carnivore, insectivore; fish, crayfish, frogs, small mammals, aquatic insects

Sounds: loud shrill cries when threatened, during play will grunt, growl and snort, chuckles when with mate or siblings

Breeding: Mar-Apr mating; 200-270 days gestation; implantation delayed for an unknown amount of time, entire reproduction process may take up to a year, female mates again days after giving birth

Young: 1-6 offspring once per year in March or April; born fully furred with eyes closed, eyes open at around 30 days, weaned at about 3 months

sleeping

Signs: haul outs, slides and rolling areas; scat is dark brown to green, short segments frequently contain fish bones and scales or crayfish parts, deposited on lakeshores, riverbanks, rocks or logs in water

scat

Activity: diurnal, nocturnal; active year-round, spends most of time in water, comes onto land to rest and sleep, curls up like a house cat to sleep

Tracks: hind paw 3½" (9 cm), forepaw slightly smaller, both round with a well-defined heel pad and toes spread evenly apart, 5 toes on all feet; 1 set of 4 tracks when bounding; 12-24" (30-61 cm) stride

Stan's Notes: A large semiaquatic animal once found in Arizona in major rivers, but wiped out (extirpated) by hunting and trapping. Reintroduction began around the state during the early 1980s. Protected in Arizona.

Well suited to life in water, with a streamlined body, webbed toes, long guard hairs and dense oily undercoat. Special valves close the nostrils underwater, enabling submersion for up to 6-8 minutes.

A playful, social animal, not often very afraid of people. Can be seen in small groups (mostly mothers with young), swimming and fishing in rivers and lakes. Frequently raises its head high while treading water to survey surroundings. Enjoys sliding on its belly down well-worn areas of mud, snow or ice (slides) on a riverbank or lakeshore just for fun. Can dive to depths of 50 feet (15 m). Sensitive to water pollution, quickly leaving a contaminated area.

Often feeds on slow-moving fish that are easy to catch such as catfish and suckers. Mistakenly blamed for eating too many game fish. Comes to the surface to eat, bringing larger items to eat at the shore. Uses its forepaws to manipulate, carry and tear apart food. Creates haul outs, well-worn trails leading from the water that often end up being littered with fish heads, scat and crayfish parts.

Likes to roll, which flattens areas of vegetation up to 6 feet (1.8 m) wide. Rolling areas have a musky odor from scent marking and usually contain some scat. Very vocal, giving a variety of sounds, such as a loud whistle, to communicate over long distances.

Male defends territory against other males. Female moves freely in and out of male territory. Digs den in a riverbank or lakeshore, often with an underwater entrance. May use an old beaver lodge. Has permanent and temporary dens. Permanent den, lined with leaves, grasses, mosses and hair, usually is where young are born.

Becomes sexually mature at 2-3 years. A male is generally solitary except during mating season and not around for the birth of the young. Returns in midsummer to help raise them.

233

Western Spotted Skunk
Spilogale gracilis

Family: Skunks (Mephitidae)

Size: L 9-12½" (23-32 cm); T 4½-7" (11-18 cm)

Weight: 1-1½ lb. (.5-.7 kg)

Description: White spot on head between eyes. Several stripes along the back and sides, some horizontal, some vertical, others broken into dashes and spots. Black tail with a white tip.

Origin/Age: native; 2-5 years

Compare: Much smaller than the Striped Skunk (pg. 247), which has a large white stripe on its back, a white tail and a narrow white stripe between its eyes.

Habitat: oak woodlands, canyons with rivers, woodland edges, shrublands, semideserts, suburban and urban areas, mountainsides, elevations up to 8,000' (2,440 m)

Home: no regular burrow, mainly a rock crevice, hollow log or tree crevice, under a deck or porch

Food: omnivore; insects, spiders, small mammals, earthworms, grubs, bird eggs, amphibians, corn, fruit, berries, nuts, seeds, reptiles

Sounds: generally quiet, will stomp front feet and exhale in a loud "pfittt," also chatters its teeth

Breeding: Sep-Oct mating; 30-33 weeks gestation; implantation delayed until 20-30 days after mating

Young: 2-6 offspring once per year in April or May; born naked with black and white skin (matching the color of its future fur coat) and eyes closed, musky odor at 8-10 days, eyes open at about 30 days

Signs: pungent odor, more obvious when the skunk has sprayed, can be detected even if it has not sprayed; small, dark, segmented cylindrical scat, deposited on trails and at the entrance to den

Activity: mostly nocturnal; more active in summer than winter

Tracks: hind paw 1½" (4 cm) long with 5 toes and a well-defined heel pad, appearing flat-footed, forepaw 1" (2.5 cm) long and wide with 5 toes; 1 set of 4 tracks when bounding; fore and hind prints are very close together, 3-5" (7.5-13 cm) stride

Stan's Notes: It was reported in the early 1900s that this species was more common than the Striped Skunk (pg. 247) in its range. Occurs throughout Arizona, but not common in any area today, with populations fluctuating widely. For reasons unknown, populations of Western Spotted Skunk and the very similar Eastern Spotted Skunk (which doesn't occur in Arizona and isn't shown) have decreased dramatically across America. For a time, Western and Eastern Spotted Skunks were considered a single species, but now they are separated into two different species. The Western is the smaller of the two and has a larger white tip on its tail.

The smallest of the skunks and also the most weasel-like in body shape and behavior. Fast, agile and adept at climbing trees. An expert mouser that, like a house cat, is good at controlling small mammal populations around ranches. Sometimes called Civet Cat, but this name is misleading because it is neither a civet (mongoose, member of the Viverridae family), nor is it a cat. Considered by some people to have the softest fur of all animals.

Much more carnivorous than the Striped Skunk. Constantly on the move, looking for its next meal. Strictly nocturnal, extremely secretive and rarely seen.

When threatened it rushes forward, stomps its feet and stands on its forepaws with hind end elevated. Agile enough to spray from this position. Able to spray as far as 10 feet (3 m) with surprising accuracy. Odor is similar to that of the Striped Skunk.

Breeds in autumn unlike other skunk species, which are spring breeders. Young are born in April and May. Young females are breeding at 4-5 months, which means they are mating by their first fall. Solitary except for breeding or when mothers have young.

Hooded Skunk
Mephitis macroura

Family: Skunks (Mephitidae)

Size: L 12-15" (30-38 cm); T 12-20" (30-50 cm)

Weight: 2-4 lb. (.9-1.8 kg)

Description: A small skunk with several color patterns. Bushy tail, equal to body length or longer, all white, all black or black with a white tip. Thin white stripe between ears and eyes. Upper neck has longer hair (ruff), like a hood. Male larger than female.

Origin/Age: native; 2-5 years

Compare: Striped Skunk (pg. 247) has a larger body, shorter tail than body length and lacks a thin white stripe down the sides. The Hog-nosed Skunk (pg. 243) has long front claws and a pig-like naked snout. The Western Spotted Skunk (pg. 235) is smaller and has a white spot between its eyes, not a stripe.

Habitat: rocky canyons, desert scrub, woodland edges, streams, elevations under 6,000' (1830 m)

Home: burrow, often in a hollow log or tree crevice, rock crevice, brush pile or small rock pile in summer

Food: omnivore; insects, worms, grubs, mammals, bird eggs, amphibians, reptiles, corn, fruit, nuts, seeds

Sounds: generally quiet, will stomp front feet and exhale in a loud "pfittt," also chatters its teeth

Breeding: Feb-Mar mating; 60-61 days gestation; implantation presumed delayed up to 2 weeks after mating

Young: 3-8 offspring once per year; born naked with black and white skin (matching the color of its future fur coat) and eyes closed, musky odor at 8-10 days, eyes open at about 24 days

239

Signs: pungent odor, more obvious when the skunk has sprayed, detectable even when it has not sprayed; segmented cylindrical scat, often dark, deposited on trails and at the entrance to the den

Activity: mostly nocturnal; more active in summer than winter

Tracks: hind paw 2-2¾" (5-7 cm) long with 5 toes and a well-defined heel pad, looking flat-footed, forepaw 1-1¾" (2.5-4.5 cm) long and wide with 5 toes; alternating fore and hind prints are very close together when walking, 4-6" (10-15 cm) stride

Stan's Notes: This species is also known as White-sided Skunk, Southern Skunk or Zorrillo. Its range runs from Central America into North America, extending throughout Mexico and reaching into the United States, where it is found only in the southern half of Arizona, southwestern New Mexico and western Texas.

The fur of Hooded Skunk is longer and softer than other skunk species. Long hairs at the base of its head make the animal appear like it is wearing a hood and are the reason for its common name.

This skunk has several color patterns. The double stripe form has a thin white stripe from the front legs to the hind quarters and a larger central white stripe running down the back from the head to the tail. The single stripe pattern is mostly white with one wide white stripe from the back of the head going down the back and extending throughout the tail. A third form has an all-black body with only thin lateral stripes and black tail with a small white tip.

Often misidentified or confused with the Striped Skunk (pg. 247) in Arizona because the two have very similar color patterns. Best to look at tail length and presence of the hood to help identify.

More nocturnal than other skunk species and also less aggressive when trapped or cornered. Often seen dead at roadsides where it was too slow to move out of the way of passing vehicles. Has the same odor as other skunks and is very closely related to both the Striped Skunk and Hog-nosed Skunk (pg. 243).

Feeds primarily on insects and consumes more plant material, such as cactus fruit and berries, than the other skunk species. It is the least studied of the skunks, which has caused its natural history information to be limited.

Hog-nosed Skunk
Conepatus leuconotus

Family: Skunks (Mephitidae)

Size: L 14-16" (36-40 cm); T 7-16" (18-40 cm)

Weight: 3-6 lb. (1.4-2.7 kg)

Description: A large skunk with a simple, sharply bicolored color pattern, black on the bottom, white on top. Long naked snout. Short powerful legs with long downward curving front claws. Lacks any white stripe or mark between eyes. All-white tail.

Origin/Age: native; 2-5 years

Compare: Unique-appearing skunk that is easily identified by its solid white back and tail and black sides and legs. Look for the long naked nose and long curved front claws to help identify.

Habitat: rocky canyons, desert scrub, mesquite grasslands, oak woodlands, below 6,000' (1,830 m)

Home: rock crevice or hollow, occasionally in a brush pile, especially in summer

Food: omnivore; mainly insects, spiders, grubs, small mammals, fruit

Sounds: generally quiet, will stomp front feet and exhale in a loud "pfittt," also chatters its teeth

Breeding: Feb-Mar mating; 59-61 days gestation; implantation presumed delayed until 2 weeks after mating

Young: 2-4 offspring once per year; born naked with black and white skin (matching the color of its future fur coat) and eyes closed, musky odor at 1-2 days

243

Signs: pungent odor, more obvious when the skunk has sprayed, detectable even when it has not sprayed; segmented cylindrical scat, often dark, deposited on trails and at the entrance to the den

Activity: mostly nocturnal; can be active during the day in winter when the days are warm and nights are very cold

Tracks: hind paw 2¼-3¼" (5.5-8 cm) long with 5 toes and a well-defined heel pad, looking flat-footed, forepaw 1-1¾" (2.5-4.5 cm) long and wide with 5 toes and distinct claw marks; alternating fore and hind prints are very close together when walking, 4-6" (10-15 cm) stride

Stan's Notes: The only skunk with an elongated naked nose and long curved front claws. Uses its claws and powerful front legs to dig up insects, which are the mainstay of its diet. This rooting behavior has given it another common name, Rooter Skunk. When actively hunting it turns soil over like a plow, leaving freshly exposed soil in its wake. Spends a lot of time in rock piles and other rocky areas where it roots around for food. Will feed on other small mammals if it can catch them.

Usually nocturnal, it can be seen hunting during the day in mid-winter. Usually avoids hot desert areas. Not very common in any part of its range. Range was once as far north as Oklahoma, but this skunk apparently isn't adapting well to habitat change. Now found only in Arizona from northwestern to southeastern parts of the state, southern New Mexico and southern Texas, extending down into Mexico. Populations have been declining dramatically all across its range.

Can be very tolerant of people, but if approach is too close it will defend itself in usual skunk-like fashion, which consists of rushing forward, stomping its feet and raising its tail just before spraying.

Was once considered two separate species known as the Eastern Hog-nosed Skunk (southern Texas and eastern Mexico) and the Western Hog-nosed Skunk (Arizona, western Texas, New Mexico and most of Mexico), but now viewed as a single species with several common names including Common Hog-nosed Skunk and White-backed Hog-nosed Skunk.

Striped Skunk
Mephitis mephitis

Family: Skunks (Mephitidae)

Size: L 20-24" (50-61 cm); T 7-14" (18-36 cm)

Weight: 6-12 lb. (2.7-5.4 kg)

Description: Variable in color, black with a large white stripe from ears to tail, sometimes splitting down the hind quarters. Large bushy tail, shorter or equal to body length, white or black with white sides. Thin white stripe going down the center of head between ears and eyes. Male larger than female.

Origin/Age: native; 2-5 years

Compare: Western Spotted Skunk (pg. 235) is smaller and has a white spot between the eyes, not a stripe. Hooded Skunk (pg. 239) has a thin white stripe on its sides and tail that is longer than its body.

Habitat: woodlands, river bottoms, fields, suburban and urban areas, mountains, up to 10,000' (3,050 m)

Home: burrow, often in hollow log or tree crevice, under a deck, porch, firewood or rock pile in summer

Food: omnivore; insects, spiders, small mammals, earthworms, grubs, bird eggs, amphibians, corn, fruit, berries, nuts, seeds, reptiles

Sounds: generally quiet, will stomp front feet and exhale in a loud "pfittt," also chatters its teeth

Breeding: Feb-Apr mating; 62-66 days gestation; implantation delayed until 18-20 days after mating

Young: 4-7 offspring once per year; born naked with black and white skin (matching the color of its future fur coat) and eyes closed, musky odor at 8-10 days, eyes open at about 24 days

Signs: pungent odor, more obvious when the skunk has sprayed, can be detected even when it has not sprayed; segmented cylindrical scat, often dark, deposited on trails and at entrance to the den

scat

Activity: mostly nocturnal; more active during summer than winter

Tracks: hind paw 2-3½" (5-9 cm) long with 5 toes and a well-defined heel pad, appearing flat-footed, forepaw 1-1¾" (2.5-4.5 cm) long and wide with 5 toes; alternating fore and hind prints are very close together when walking, 4-6" (10-15 cm) stride

Stan's Notes: Striped Skunk occurs across the United States and well into Canada. It can be highly variable in color and pattern across this large range; however, in Arizona it has a unique color pattern. The Arizona form often has a wide white stripe extending from the head down the back and to the tail. The tail is often all white or black with white edges. Tail length is shorter or about the same length as the body, unlike the Hooded Skunk (pg. 239), which has a tail longer than its body.

Bred in the early 1900s for its fur, which explains the wide variety of colors in pet skunks today. The white stripes of a skunk, which vary in length and width from one animal to another, can be used to identify individuals. Some have such wide stripes that they appear to be all white, although most are not albino.

The prominent black and white markings warn predators that it should not be approached. Will face a predator when threatened, arch its back and raise its tail while chattering its teeth. If this does not deter the predator, it will rush forward, stomp its feet, stand on forepaws with tail elevated and spray an oily, odorous yellow substance from glands at the base of its tail near the anus.

Able to spray 5-6 times up to 15 feet (4.6 m) with surprising accuracy. This substance can cause temporary blindness and intense pain if it enters the eyes. Holding the animal by its tail off the ground will not prevent it from spraying. Genus and species names refer to the spray and mean "bad odor."

This is a solitary, secretive skunk that wanders around in a slow, shuffling waddle in search of food. Does not hibernate, but will hole up in its burrow for several weeks to two months during cold, snowy weather. Has been known to burrow in groups of up to 15 individuals, often all females. This can be a problem when the burrow is under a house because of the cumulative smell.

Ringtail
Bassariscus astutus

Family: Raccoons (Procyonidae)

Size: L 12-15½" (30-39 cm); T 12-16" (30-40 cm)

Weight: 2-2½ lb. (.9-1.1 kg)

Description: Cat-like in shape. Overall yellowish gray with long dark guard hairs, giving it a grizzled appearance. Small head with large pointed ears, like a fox. Very large dark eyes with a white ring around each eye. Large tail with 7-8 black and white or brown and white rings and a black tip.

Origin/Age: native; 6-10 years

Compare: Smaller and thinner than the Northern Raccoon (pg. 255), which has a distinctive black mask and shorter tail. Much smaller than White-nosed Coati (pg. 259), which has smaller eyes and ears and much less distinct rings on tail.

Habitat: canyonlands, semideserts, scrublands, elevations up to 9,000' (2,745 m)

Home: hollow tree, rock crevices, or underground den where trees are absent, den is lined with grasses and leaves

Food: omnivore; crayfish, fish, reptiles, amphibians, nuts, fruit, green leaves, suet, bird eggs, insects, small mammals such as mice, ground squirrels and baby birds

Sounds: snarls, growls and barks as alarm and threat calls

Breeding: Feb-Jun mating; 54-65 days gestation; female in heat (estrus) for only 3-6 days

Young: 1-5 offspring once per year, often in May or June; born with eyes closed, leaves den at 7-8 weeks

Signs: elongated cylindrical scat of various sizes and shapes, often placed in just one place, creating large common latrines to mark territories

Activity: nocturnal; active year-round except during cold snaps in winter

Tracks: hind paw 2¼-3" (5.5-7.5 cm) long with 5 long toes and no claw marks, forepaw 1½-2" (4-5 cm) long, slightly longer than wide with 5 distinct toes and no claw marks; tracks rarely seen because of the rocky habitat

Stan's Notes: A unique animal in Arizona that has a body like a cat, face and ears like a fox, a tail like a raccoon and climbs like a squirrel. An excellent mouser, once captured to control rodent populations in mines and referred to as Miner's Cat. Also known as Ringtail Cat, Civet Cat or Rock Cat. Another common name, Cacomistle, coming from the Mexican Nahuatl Indians, translates to "half mountain lion."

This animal is an excellent climber, with sharp claws that facilitate climbing trees and large rocks. The hind feet rotate 180 degrees, allowing it to climb down trees and rocks like a squirrel, face first. Can also jump across great distances, similar to squirrels.

A nocturnal critter and an expert hunter, bringing down a wide variety of mice, ground squirrels, woodrats and other small mammals, along with lizards and large insects. Pounces on prey and kills it, biting the base of the neck, and eats meals headfirst.

Not much is known about the distribution. Recent studies find it more widespread and possibly more common than previously noted. Unknown social structure, but some individuals hunt and travel together where ranges overlap.

Males mark their territories with urine. Anal glands in both sexes give off a foul odor when the animal is threatened or alarmed.

Northern Raccoon
Procyon lotor

Family: Raccoons (Procyonidae)

Size: L 24-25" (61-64 cm); T 7-16" (18-40 cm)

Weight: 12-35 lb. (5.4-15.8 kg)

Description: Overall gray to brown, sometimes nearly black to silver. Distinctive black band across face (mask), eyes and down to the chin. White snout. Bushy, black-tipped brown tail with 4-6 evenly spaced dark bands or rings.

Origin/Age: native; 6-10 years

Compare: Very distinctive animal. The black mask and dark rings on the tail make it hard to confuse with any other species.

Habitat: almost all habitats, rural and urban, elevations up to 10,000' (3,050 m)

Home: hollow tree, or underground den where trees are absent

Food: omnivore; crayfish, fish, reptiles, amphibians, nuts, fruit, green leaves, suet, birdseed (especially black-oil sunflower seeds and thistle), small mammals, baby birds, bird eggs, insects

Sounds: very loud snarls, growls, hisses and screams are common (and may be frightening) during the mating season, soft purring sounds and quiet chuckles between mothers and babies

Breeding: Feb-Jun mating; 54-65 days gestation; female in heat (estrus) for only 3-6 days

Young: 3-6 offspring per year, usually in May; born with eyes closed, leaves den at 7-8 weeks

Signs: pile of half-digested berries deposited on a log, rock, under a bird feeder or on top of a garbage can; scat is usually cylindrical, 2" (5 cm) long and ¾" (2 cm) wide, but can be highly variable due to diet

scat

Activity: nocturnal; active year-round except during cold snaps in winter

Tracks: hind paw 3½-4½" (9-11 cm) long with 5 long toes and claw marks, forepaw 2½-3" (6-7.5 cm) long, slightly longer than wide with 5 distinct toes and claw marks; forepaws land (register) next to hind prints, 8-20" (20-50 cm) stride

Stan's Notes: Raccoons are native only to the Americas from Central America to the United States and lower Canada. Northern Raccoon is found in various parts of Arizona. Common name comes from the Algonquian Indian word *arougbcoune*, meaning "he scratches with his hands." Known for the ability to open such objects as doors, coolers and latches. Uses its nimble fingers to feel around the edges of ponds, rivers and lakes for crayfish and frogs. Known to occasionally wash its food before eating, hence the species name *lotor*, meaning "washer." However, it is not washing its food, but kneading and tearing it apart. The water helps it feel the parts that are edible and those that are not. A strong swimmer.

juveniles

Able to climb any tree very quickly and can come down headfirst or tail end first. Its nails can grip bark no matter which way it climbs because it can rotate its hind feet nearly 180 degrees so that the hind toes always point up the tree.

Active at night, sleeping in hollow trees or other dens during the day. Often mistakenly associated with forests, but also lives in grasslands, using underground dens.

Usually a solitary animal as an adult. Does not hibernate but will sleep or simply hole up in a comfortable den from January to February. Will occasionally den in small groups of the same sex, usually males, or females without young.

Emerging from winter sleep, males wander many miles in search of a mate. Females use the same den for several months while raising their young, but move out afterward and find a new place to sleep each night. Males are not involved in raising young. Young remain with the adult female for nearly a year.

White-nosed Coati
Nasua narica

Family: Raccoons (Procyonidae)

Size: L 25-30" (64-76 cm); T 15-27" (38-69 cm)

Weight: 10-25 lb. (4.5-11.3 kg)

Description: Overall light to dark brown, frequently cinnamon, sometimes with a lighter saddle-like shape on the back. Distinctive black marks on face with white around eyes and a white snout. Short round ears. Short legs with white on upper part of front legs. Long curved claws. A very long, bushy tail with faint rings, tapering to a point at the end. Often holds tail up straight or bent like a question mark.

Origin/Age: native; 6-10 years

Compare: Northern Raccoon (pg. 255) has a black mask and shorter tail with rings on it. Ringtail (pg. 251) is much smaller, with a bushier, dark-ringed tail.

Habitat: mountain forests, wooded canyons, often near water, elevations up to 11,500' (3,510 m)

Home: no real home or den, spends the night in trees, daytime on the ground; uses a maternity den in a rock outcrop for birthing

Food: omnivore; fruit, nuts, large insects, amphibians, reptiles, small mammals, baby birds, bird eggs

Sounds: very loud growls and snarls, hisses and whimpers, soft chattering and chirps

Breeding: Jan-Mar mating; 75-77 days gestation

Young: 4-6 offspring once per year, in spring; born with eyes closed, leaves the den at 5-6 weeks, young have darker coats than adults, young males stay with the troop until 2 years of age

259

sleeping

Signs: pile of half-digested berries deposited on a log or rock; scat is usually cylindrical, 2" (5 cm) long and ¾" (2 cm) wide, but can be highly variable depending on diet

Activity: diurnal; active year-round, sleeps in trees at night

Tracks: hind paw 3-3½" (7.5-9 cm) long with 5 long toes and claw marks, forepaw 2-2½" (5-6 cm) long with 5 distinct toes and very long claw marks; forepaws land (register) behind the hind prints, 7-15" (18-38 cm) stride

Stan's Notes: A very interesting relative to the more common and well-known raccoon. Also known as Antoon, Coatimundi or just Coati (pronounced "ko-WHA-tee"). Often called Tejon ("badger") in Mexico. All members of the Raccoons family live in the New World. The coati is found in Mexico and Central America, with small populations in Arizona and along the Texas border. Isolated populations occurring in southern California and Florida may be the South American Coati (*N. nasua*) (not shown), a different species with a dark snout and distinct rings on its tail.

Active during the day, foraging for food in large groups. A group, or troop, consists of up to 50 females and young, but smaller sizes are more common. Males are solitary except for a few weeks during breeding season when they seek receptive females.

Feeds by rooting around in leaf litter for insects, nuts and berries. Climbs trees for fruit and often returns repeatedly until all fruit is gone. A true omnivore, eating whatever food it finds. Feeds in the morning and late in the evening, napping and grooming during the day, especially when it is hot.

Swims well and is an excellent climber, using its long tail to help balance on small branches. Travels holding its tail upright and lowers tail when feeding.

Sleeps in trees at night to avoid predators. Active all year and does not use a den except when giving birth. Females will use the den with their young for the first 5-6 weeks until the young are strong enough to keep up with the troop.

More gregarious than other members of the Raccoons family and much more vocal. Young play noisily, while adults are most vocal when interacting with each other. Spends time grooming itself and other individuals while giving soft soothing sounds.

Like the raccoon, the coati tolerates people well and will raid camps, garbage cans and parking lots for anything edible. Highly intelligent and able to problem solve and remember tasks.

North American Porcupine
Erethizon dorsatum

Family: Porcupine (Erethizontidae)

Size: L 20-26" (50-66 cm); T 6-12" (15-30 cm)

Weight: 7-30 lb. (3.2-13.5 kg)

Description: A short, stocky body with short legs, an arching back and quills on rump and tail. Dark brown to nearly black. Longest guard hairs are often white-tipped. Ears are small, round and barely visible. Tiny dark eyes. Small feet with long claws.

Origin/Age: native; 5-10 years

Compare: Similar size as Striped Skunk (pg. 247), but lacks white stripes. Look for the obvious body shape (arching back) and large white-tipped quills to identify. Can be seen on the ground or in trees.

Habitat: coniferous and deciduous forests, yards, grasslands, up to the tree line at 10,000' (3,050 m)

Home: den in a large hollow tree or a fallen hollow log, underground burrow

Food: herbivore; soft bark, inner bark of conifers, green plants, tree leaves, leaf buds

Sounds: much vocalization with loud, shrill screeching during mating, mothers make soft grunts and groans to communicate with their babies

Breeding: Oct-Nov mating; 7 months gestation; female is receptive to mating (estrus) for only 8-12 hours; has a very long gestation period for a rodent

Young: 1 offspring once per year in May or June; born fully quilled with teeth erupted and eyes open, feeds itself within 1 week, weaned by 1 month, stays with mother until the first autumn

263

juvenile

Signs: large pieces of bark gnawed from coniferous trunks, tooth marks on exposed wood, cleanly chewed twigs and branches laying nearby, chew marks on buildings, canoe paddles and ax handles; pile of pellets, often irregular in size and shape due to diet, may have soft segmented scat in summer, hard individual pellets in winter

scat

Activity: mostly nocturnal, crepuscular; active year-round

Tracks: hind paw 3-3½" (7.5-9 cm) long, wide oval with claw marks and dotted (stippled) impression from rough, pebbled pads, forepaw 2-2½" (5-6 cm) long, oval with claw marks; 1 set of 2 tracks; fore and hind prints alternate left and right with toes pointing inward, hind paws fall near or onto fore prints, tail drag mark between each set of prints in mud or deep snow

Stan's Notes: A slow, solitary animal that is usually seen sleeping at the top of a tree or slowly crossing a road. Makes up for its slow speed by protecting itself with long, barb-tipped guard hairs that are solid at the tip and base and hollow in between. It has over 30,000 sharp quills, which actually are modified hairs loosely attached to a sheet of muscles just beneath the skin. Unable to throw the quills, but will swing and hit with its tail, driving the tail quills deep into even the toughest flesh. Some report that quill barbs are heat sensitive and open when entering flesh, making them very hard to extract. Quills provide such an excellent defense, only few predators are capable of killing a porcupine.

Uses a den in a large tree for sleeping during the day or for holing up for several days or weeks during cold snaps in winter. Feeds on inner bark of coniferous trees in winter, but moves to the ground to eat green vegetation in spring and summer.

Males find females during the mating season by sniffing the base of trees and rocks where a female might have passed. Males can become very aggressive toward other males, often fighting during the breeding season.

Elaborate mating with much vocalization and several males often attending one female. When the female is ready to mate, she will raise her tail to permit typical mounting.

Babies have an atypical birth, emerging headfirst with eyes open, teeth erupted and body covered with soft, flexible quills. Quills dry and become stiff within a couple hours.

Virginia Opossum
Didelphis virginiana

RARE

Family: Opossums (Didelphidae)

Size: L 25-30" (64-76 cm); T 10-20" (25-50 cm)

Weight: 4-14 lb. (1.8-6.3 kg)

Description: Overall black. Some have a gray-to-brown body with a white head, throat and belly. Long narrow snout. Wide mouth. Oval, naked black ears and a pink nose. Short legs and 5 pink toes on feet. Thumb-like first toe on the hind feet lacks a nail. Long, scaly, semiprehensile, naked pinkish tail.

Origin/Age: non-native, from eastern United States; 3-5 years

Compare: Muskrat (pg. 101) is much smaller, all brown and rarely far from water. Norway Rat (pg. 91) also has a long naked tail, but Virginia Opossum is larger with large dark ears and a pink nose. Norway Rat is rarely seen in trees.

Habitat: deciduous forests, farmlands, grasslands, cities, yards, elevations up to 6,000' (1,830 m)

Home: leaf nest in an underground den or hollow log

Food: omnivore; insects, sunflower and Nyjer thistle seeds, nuts, berries, fruit, leaves, bird eggs, fish, reptiles, amphibians, small mammals, road kill, earthworms

Sounds: low growls, hisses and shows teeth if threatened, soft clicks between mothers and young

Breeding: Jan-Feb mating; 8-14 days gestation

Young: 2-13 (usually 5-6) offspring once per year; newborns the size of a navy bean crawl to mother's external fur-lined pouch, where they attach to a nipple for as long as 2 months

Sonoran

Sonoran

scat

Signs: overturned garbage cans; scat on ground under sunflower seed and Nyjer thistle feeders

Activity: nocturnal; can be seen during the day in winter

Tracks: hind paw 2" (5 cm) long with 5 toes, large thumb-like first toe points inward and lacks a nail, forepaw 1½" (4 cm) long with 5 toes spread out; fore and hind prints are parallel, 7" (18 cm) stride, often has a tail drag mark

Stan's Notes: The Virginia Opossum was introduced to Arizona in the early 1900s and is seen only in the southeastern part of the state. The Sonoran Opossum, a dark, nearly black variety with black feet and a black mask, moved into Arizona from Mexico and over the past two decades has become more common. Other than the overall color, there is not much difference between the Virginia and the Sonoran.

A unique-looking animal, the size of a house cat. It has 50 teeth, more than any other mammal in Arizona. In some areas the tip of its naked pink tail and ears get frostbitten during winter, turn black and fall off.

Usually solitary, moving around on the ground from place to place. Also climbs trees well, using its tail to aid in climbing, holding onto branches (semiprehensile). An adult opossum cannot hang by the tail like a monkey, but the young seem able to, perhaps due to their lighter weight.

Frequently feeds on dead animals along roads and is often hit by vehicles. Not a fast mover, it will hiss if threatened and show its short, pointy teeth. When that doesn't work, it often will roll over and feign death with eyes closed, mouth open and tongue hanging out, "playing 'possum." Does not hibernate, but sleeps in dens for weeks during the coldest part of winter.

Males give loud, aggressive displays during the breeding season and will scent-mark by licking themselves and rubbing their heads against tree trunks or other stationary objects. Young ride on their mother's back after weaning.

Opossums can defend themselves against large predators and survive substantial injuries. One study showed nearly half of all examined dead opossums had healed broken bones, some with multiple fractures. Many opossums are immune to venomous snake bites and have a resistance to rabies and plague.

Kit Fox
Vulpes macrotis

Family: Wolves, Foxes and Coyote (Canidae)

Size: L 15-21" (38-53 cm); T 9-12" (23-30 cm); H 10-12" (25-30 cm)

Weight: 3-7 lb. (1.4-3.2 kg)

Description: Yellowish tan fox with a dark line down the back and onto tail. White chin and upper neck. White to tan on the belly. Extremely large, pointed ears. Long thin legs, same color as the body.

Origin/Age: native, 5-10 years

Compare: The Gray Fox (pg. 275) is larger, darker and has shorter ears. Red Fox (pg. 279) is larger and has red fur with a white-tipped tail.

Habitat: deserts, semideserts, canyons, grasslands, open fields, elevations below 6,000' (1,830 m)

Home: underground den, sometimes a hollow log or in a hillside or stream bank, with 3-4 entrances, often with a dirt mound up to 3' (.9 m) high with scat and scraps of food in front of main entrance; may have several den sites in its territory

Food: omnivore; small mammals such as rabbits, hares, mice, woodrats and voles; also eats fish, berries, apples, nuts, insects and carrion

Sounds: hoarse high-pitched barks, yelps to steady high-pitched screams, mournful cries

Breeding: winter (Jan-Mar) mating; 51-53 days gestation

Young: 1-8 kits once per year in April or May

Signs: cylindrical scat with a tapered end, frequently contains hair and bones, often found on a trail, prominent rock or stump or at the den entrance

Activity: mainly nocturnal, crepuscular; active around the den site at sunrise and sunset, but can also be seen there during the day, sunning itself

Tracks: forepaw 1½" (4 cm) long, oval, with hind paw slightly smaller; 4 toes on each foot, straight line of single tracks; hind paws fall near or directly onto fore prints (direct register) when walking, often obliterating the forepaw tracks, 8-12" (20-30 cm) stride when walking

Stan's Notes: Federally listed as an endangered species. Numbers were reduced in the past by loss of habitat and excessive trapping for its fur. Range extends from California, Nevada and Arizona to New Mexico and farther south into Mexico. Once considered the same species as Swift Fox (not shown), which is not in Arizona.

Considered the smallest of our wild dogs, with the approximate size of a house cat. A highly specialized fox, surviving in both desert and semidesert environments. Does not require a constant supply of fresh water, obtaining all the moisture it needs from its prey and by water conservation, achieved through the production of a specialized urine that is low in water content.

Diet consists of small rodents such as kangaroo rats, but will also take rabbits. Fleet of foot, it runs very fast for short distances, allowing it to capture other swift prey such as hares.

Digs it own den (semifossorial) down as far as 8 feet (2.4 m), fashioning it with many entrances. Doesn't hibernate. Mates pair up in late winter when females clean out dens and get ready to breed. Young first emerge at the den entrance at 5-6 weeks of age. Some report that helper females take part in raising the young of older females.

Some pairs have long-term pair bonds; others don't. Males will bring food to the female while she is nursing young. At weaning, both adults hunt for food and bring it back to the den. Parents carry prey whole to the den and don't regurgitate food.

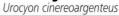
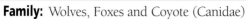

Gray Fox
Urocyon cinereoargenteus

Family: Wolves, Foxes and Coyote (Canidae)

Size: L 22-24" (56-61 cm); T 10-17" (25-43 cm); H 14-15" (36-38 cm)

Weight: 7-13 lb. (3.2-5.9 kg)

Description: Grizzled gray fox with a rust red nape, shoulders and rust red across the chest. Large pointed ears, trimmed in white. White chin, neck and belly. Large bushy tail with a black tip and ridge of stiff dark hairs along the top.

Origin/Age: native; 5-10 years

Compare: The Red Fox (pg. 279) has a white-tipped tail. Coyote (pg. 283) shares the grayish appearance and black-tipped tail, but is larger than the Gray Fox and has longer legs.

Habitat: desert scrub, forests, rocky outcrops, river valleys, brush areas, elevations up to 7,500' (2,285 m)

Home: den, mostly in a natural cavity such as a log or a crevice in rock, will enlarge a prairie dog burrow, unlike a Red Fox den, the den of a Gray Fox lacks a mound of dirt in front of the entrance

Food: omnivore; small mammals such as mice, voles, rabbits and hares; also eats berries, apples, nuts, fish, insects and carrion

Sounds: hoarse high-pitched barks, yelps to steady high-pitched screams, mournful cries; much less vocal than the Red Fox

Breeding: winter (Jan-Mar) mating; 51-53 days gestation

Young: 1-7 kits once per year in April or May; born helpless with black fur and eyes closed

Signs: urine and piles of feces, mostly on conspicuous landmarks such as a prominent rock, stump or trail; cylindrical scat with a tapered end, can be very dark if berries were eaten, often contains hair and bones

scat

Activity: mostly nocturnal, crepuscular; can be seen during the day in winter, especially when overcast

Tracks: forepaw 1½" (4 cm) long, oval, hind paw slightly smaller; straight line of single tracks; hind paws fall near or directly onto fore prints (direct register) when walking, often obliterating the forepaw tracks, 10-14" (25-36 cm) stride when walking

Stan's Notes: This is by far the most common fox species in Arizona. The scientific name provides a very good description of the animal. The genus name *Urocyon* is Greek for "tailed dog." The species *cinereoargenteus* is Latin and means "silver" or "gray and black."

Also called Treefox because it often climbs trees. Climbs to escape larger predators more than it does to find food. Sometimes it will rest in a tree. Shinnies up, pivoting its front legs at the shoulder joints to grab the trunk and pushes with hind feet. Able to rotate its front legs more than other canids. Once up the trunk, it jumps from branch to branch and has been seen up to 20 feet (6.1 m) high. Descends by backing down or running headfirst down a sloping branch.

Thought to mate for life. Male often travels 50 miles (81 km) to establish territory. A pair will defend a territory of 2-3 square miles (5-8 sq. km).

The kits are weaned at about six weeks. Male doesn't enter the den, but helps feed the family by bringing in food. Young disperse at the end of summer just before the parents start mating again.

Red Fox
Vulpes vulpes

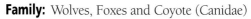

Family: Wolves, Foxes and Coyote (Canidae)

Size: L 22-24" (56-61 cm); T 13-17" (33-43 cm); H 15-16" (38-40 cm)

Weight: 7-15 lb. (3.2-6.8 kg)

Description: Usually rusty red with dark highlights, but can vary from light yellow to black. Large pointed ears trimmed in black with white inside. White jowls, chest and belly. Legs nearly black. Large bushy tail with a white tip. Fluffy coat in winter and spring. Molts by July, appearing smaller and thinner.

Origin/Age: native, 5-10 years

Compare: Gray Fox (pg. 275) is not as red and has a black-tipped tail. Smaller than the Coyote (pg. 283), usually more red and has a white-tipped tail. All other wild canids lack a tail with a white tip.

Habitat: forests, scrublands, rangelands, cities, suburbs, foothills, mountains, all elevations

Home: den, sometimes a hollow log, may dig a den under a log or a rock in a bank of a stream or in a hillside created when land was cut to build a road, often has a mound of dirt up to 3' (.9 m) high in front of the main entrance with scat deposits

Food: omnivore; small mammals such as mice, voles, rabbits and hares; also eats berries, apples, nuts, fish, insects and carrion

Sounds: hoarse high-pitched barks, yelps to steady high-pitched screams, mournful cries

Breeding: winter (Jan-Mar) mating; 51-53 days gestation

Young: 1-10 kits once per year in April or May

summer coat

winter coat

silver morph

dark morph

scat

Signs: cylindrical scat with a tapered end, can be very dark if berries were eaten, frequently contains hair and bones, often found on a trail, prominent rock or stump or at den entrance

Activity: mainly nocturnal, crepuscular; rests during the middle of the night

Tracks: forepaw 2" (5 cm) long, oval, with hind paw slightly smaller; straight line of single tracks; hind paws fall near or directly onto fore prints (direct register) when walking, often obliterating the forepaw tracks, 10-14" (25-36 cm) stride when walking

Stan's Notes: The most widely distributed of wild canids in the world, ranging across North America, Asia, Europe and northern Africa. European Red Foxes were introduced into North America in the 1790s, resulting in some confusion regarding the original distribution and lineage.

Usually alone. Very intelligent and learns from past experiences. Often catlike in behavior, pouncing on prey. Sleeps at the base of a tree or rock, even in winter, curling itself up into a ball.

den entrance

Hunts for mice and other small prey by stalking, looking and listening. Hearing differs from the other mammals. Hears low-frequency sounds, enabling it to detect small mammals digging and gnawing underground. Chases larger prey such as rabbits and squirrels. Hunts even if full, caching extra food underground. Finds cached food by memory and using its sense of smell.

Mated pairs will actively defend their territory from other foxes; however, they are often killed by coyotes or wolves. Uses a den only several weeks for birthing and raising young. Parents bring food to kits in the den. At first, parents regurgitate the food. Later, they will bring fresh meat and live prey to the den, allowing the kits to practice killing. Young are dispersed at the end of their first summer, with the males (dog foxes) traveling 100-150 miles (161-242 km), much farther than females (vixens), to establish their own territories.

kits

Coyote
Canis latrans

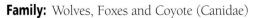

Family: Wolves, Foxes and Coyote (Canidae)

Size: L 3-3½' (.9-1.1 m); T 12-15" (30-38 cm); H 18-24" (45-61 cm)

Weight: 20-40 lb. (9-18 kg)

Description: Tan fur with black and orange highlights. Large, pointed reddish orange ears with white interior. Long narrow snout with a white upper lip. Long legs and bushy black-tipped tail.

Origin/Age: native; 5-10 years

Compare: Smaller than Mexican Wolf (pg. 287), with larger ears and a narrower pointed snout. The Red Fox (pg. 279) has black legs and a white-tipped tail.

Habitat: urban to suburban to rural areas, deserts, scrublands, mountains, forests, fields, farms, elevations up to 12,000' (3,660 m)

Home: den, usually in a riverbank, hillside, under a rock or tree root, entrance 12-24" (30-61 cm) high, can be up to 30' (9.1 m) deep and ends in small chamber where female gives birth; female may dig own den or enlarge a fox or badger den

Food: omnivore; small mammals, reptiles, amphibians, birds, bird eggs, insects, fruit, carrion

Sounds: barks like a dog, calls to others result in a chorus of high-pitched howling and yipping; sounds different from the lower, deeper call of Mexican Wolf, which rarely yips

Breeding: mid to late winter; 63 days average gestation

Young: 4-6 pups once per year in April or May; born with eyes closed

283

summer coat

winter coat

Signs: cylindrical scat (shape is similar to that of domestic dog excrement), often containing fur and bones, along well-worn game trails, on prominent rocks and at trail intersections

scat

Activity: nocturnal, crepuscular, diurnal; can be seen for several hours after sunrise and before sunset

Tracks: forepaw 2¼" (5.5 cm) long, round to slightly oval, hind paw slightly smaller; straight line of single tracks; hind paws fall near or directly onto fore prints (direct register) when walking, often obliterating the forepaw tracks, 12-15" (30-38 cm) stride when walking, 24-30" (61-76 cm) stride when running

Stan's Notes: Sometimes called Brush Wolf or Prairie Wolf, even though this animal is obviously not a wolf. The genus name *Canis* is Latin for "dog." The species name *latrans* is also Latin and means "barking." It is believed that the common name "Coyote" comes from the Aztec word *coyotl*, which means "barking dog."

Frequently seen as a gluttonous outlaw, this animal is only guilty of being able to survive a rapidly changing environment and outright slaughter by people. Intelligent and playful, much like the domestic dog. Hunts alone or in small groups. Uses its large ears to hear small mammals beneath vegetation. Stands over a spot, cocks its head back and forth to pinpoint prey and then pounces. Will also chase larger prey such as rabbits.

Most coyotes run with their tails down unlike dogs and wolves, which run with their tails level to upright. A fast runner, it can travel 25-30 mph (40-48 km/h). May reach 40 mph (64 km/h) for short distances. Some coyotes tracked with radio collars are known to travel more than 400 miles (644 km) over several days.

Often courts for 2-3 months before mating. A monogamous animal, with mated pairs staying together for many years or for life.

Pups emerge from the den at 2-3 weeks and are weaned at 5-7 weeks. Mother will move her pups from the den when she feels threatened. Mother often gets help raising young from other group members and her mate. Pups do not return to the den once they are able to survive on their own. Mother abandons the den once the pups leave and will often return year after year in spring to use the same den.

Mexican Wolf
Canis lupus baileyi

RARE

Family: Wolves, Foxes and Coyote (Canidae)

Size: L 4-5' (1.2-1.5 m); T 14-20" (36-50 cm); H 26-38" (66-96 cm)

Weight: 50-80 lb. (23-36 kg)

Description: Usually gray with dark highlights, but can vary from all white to entirely black. A large bushy tail, almost always black-tipped. Short pointed ears. Long legs. Male is slightly larger than female.

Origin/Age: native; 5-15 years

Compare: Larger than Coyote (pg. 283) and has longer legs and shorter ears. Often holds its tail straight out when traveling compared with the Coyote, which holds its tail at a downward angle.

Habitat: deciduous and coniferous forests, grasslands

Home: shelter or den only for raising young, den can be 5-15' (1.5-4.5 m) deep, frequently more than 1 entrance, fan of dirt at entrance, often scattered bones and fur laying about; used for many years

Food: omnivore; small to large mammals such as mice, rabbits, hares, deer and bears; also eats berries, grass, insects and fish

Sounds: yelps, barks and howls, howling may rise and fall in pitch or remain the same; rarely has a series of yips or yelps at the end, like the Coyote

Breeding: Jan-Feb mating; 63-65 days gestation

Young: 1-8 pups once per year; born helpless with eyes closed, wide range of color variations, some look like the parents, others are completely different, remains the same color its entire life

Signs: scrapes in the dirt, urine on posts, rocks and stumps; scat looks like the excrement of a domestic dog, but it is larger and contains hairs and bone fragments

scat

Activity: nocturnal, more diurnal in winter; hunts at night in summer

Tracks: forepaw 4½-5½" (11-14 cm) long, hind paw slightly smaller, both round with clear claw marks; straight line of single tracks; hind paws fall near or directly onto fore prints (direct register) when walking, often obliterating the forepaw tracks, 15-30" (38-76 cm) stride; rarely walks along roads like a domestic dog

Stan's Notes: The largest wild dog. The Mexican Wolf that occurs in Arizona is actually a slightly smaller and more lightweight sub-species of the Gray Wolf (*C. lupus*). Once seen across the nation, wolves were exterminated from most places. The Mexican Wolf was reintroduced into eastern Arizona starting in 1998, with the first litter born in the wild from wild parents occurring in 2002. As of 2007 there were only about 50-60 Mexican Wolves in the wild between Arizona and New Mexico.

One of the most mobile animals, traveling great distances to find food each day. Eats 3-5 pounds (1.4-2.3 kg) of meat per day, but can go weeks without food. May cache large prey items. Not a good long distance runner, but able to achieve speeds of 30 mph (48 km/h) for short distances. A good swimmer, following prey into the water. Communicates by howling, body posturing and scent marking.

Shies away from people, but this is a social animal, living in packs of 2-15 individuals that consist primarily of family members. The pack has a well-defined hierarchy with a sole male leader called alpha and his female mate, also alpha.

Territory of a pack covers 100-300 square miles (260-780 sq. km). Often uses the same well-worn trails in some areas. Territories of other packs may overlap. Conflicts rarely occur if food is plentiful.

Packs chase down prey or ambush. Dominant members feed first. Some adults bring food back in their stomachs to pups, since the mothers won't leave them the first month. Pups mob feeder adults and lick their faces, encouraging regurgitation. When the pups are older, some wolves baby-sit while the alpha pair goes hunting with the pack. Young join the pack to hunt in the fall of their first year and leave at 2-3 years to form their own pack or join another. After the pups leave, the pack will rendezvous before and after hunting, usually at a grassy area with a good view of the surroundings.

Ocelot
Leopardus pardalis

RARE

Family: Cats (Felidae)

Size: L 24-27" (61-69 cm); T 10-16" (25-40 cm); H 15-22" (38-56 cm)

Weight: 15-30 lb. (6.8-13.5 kg)

Description: Overall tan to dull yellow and covered in black spots, rings, speckles, stripes, bars or elongated thick marks with tan centers. Small head. Narrow stripes on head, neck and chest. Large round ears with a single white spot on the back of each ear. White markings near the eyes. Some individuals may have pale white cheeks. Long tail with heavy black spots.

Origin/Age: native; 7-15 years

Compare: Much smaller than Jaguar (pg. 307), which has a large head and more rings than spots. Jaguarundi (pg. 295) lacks any spots. The Bobcat (pg. 299) is much more common, has tufts on its ears and lacks the pronounced spots.

Habitat: many habitats including forests, fields, farmlands, elevations up to 12,000' (3,660 m)

Home: den for birthing, often a hollow log, rock crevice or under a pile of tree branches filled with leaves

Food: carnivore; small mammals such as mice, squirrels, rabbits, birds, reptiles, amphibians

Sounds: usually silent, but gives typical cat-like sounds in response to danger or threats, meows and yowls

Breeding: Jun-Jul mating; 80-85 days gestation

Young: 1-3 kittens once per year in September and October; born blind, leaves den after 3-4 weeks

Signs: claw scratches on a post up to 3-4' (.9-1.2 m) tall, scent posts marked with urine; cylindrical scat up to 2-3" (5-7.5 cm) long and ½" (1 cm) wide, contains hair and bones

Activity: nocturnal, diurnal; rests for several hours during the day, especially if it is hot, in a sheltered spot such as under a fallen log, beneath a shrub or in a rock crevice

Tracks: forepaw and hind paw 2-2½" (5-6 cm), round, heel pad smooth, toes evenly spread, lacking claw marks; straight line of tracks; hind paws fall near or onto fore prints (direct register) when walking, often obliterating the forepaw tracks, 9-10" (23-25 cm) stride

Stan's Notes: A very uncommon cat species in Arizona, having estimates of fewer than a couple hundred individuals. Almost all have come up from Mexico looking for new territory and hunting opportunities. Constantly on the move in search of food. Adapts to a wide variety of habitats from rainforest to open desert. Some form of cover is about the only requirement.

Breeding takes place year-round in tropical regions, with females becoming sexually mature at 18 months. Females provide all parental care. It is believed that in Arizona breeding takes place in the summer, with 1-2 young, rarely 3, produced during fall. Polygynous, males mate with all females in or near their territory.

The males have larger territories than the females, 7 square miles (18 sq. km). Females occupy 4⅓ square miles (11 sq. km), but range size varies and depends on the available food supply.

Best known for its pelt, which was the mainstay of the fur trade for many years. At one time more than 200,000 ocelots per year were killed to make coats from their pelts. Today laws prohibit hunting for the fur trade and ocelot coats are a thing of the past.

Primarily nocturnal and solitary, it is occasionally confused with domestic house cats. Mice and other small rodents are the main diet and hunting for them takes place at night. Sometimes it will take a bird, but since most birds are inactive at night this is much less common.

mother and kittens

Jaguarundi
Herpailurus yagouaroundi

RARE

Family: Cats (Felidae)

Size: L 27-33" (69-84 cm); T 12-20" (30-50 cm); H 13-19" (33-48 cm)

Weight: 10-20 lb. (4.5-9 kg)

Description: A uniformly colored cat that occurs in 2 distinct colors, reddish brown or gray, which sometimes appears black. Small, flattened, elongated head and small pointed ears. Long tail, matching the color of fur on the body. Silver-tipped fur of the dark morph gives it a grizzled appearance.

Origin/Age: native; 7-15 years

Compare: Similar size as Bobcat (pg. 299), which is much more common, has tufts on its ears and lacks the long tail. Ocelot (pg. 291) is similar in size, but has spots.

Habitat: many habitats, forests, fields ranchlands, mountains, elevations up to 8,000' (2,440 m)

Home: den for giving birth, often in a hollow log, rock crevice or under a pile of tree branches filled with leaves

Food: carnivore; small mammals such as mice, squirrels, rabbits, birds, reptiles, amphibians

Sounds: usually silent, but gives typical cat-like sounds in response to danger or threats, meows and yowls

Breeding: any time of year; 65-70 days gestation

Young: 1-3 (usually 2) kittens 1-2 times per year

dark morph

Signs: claw scratches on posts up to 24-36" (30-91 cm) tall, scent posts marked with urine; cylindrical scat up to 1-2" (2.5-5 cm) long and ¼" (.6 cm) wide, contains hair and bones

Activity: nocturnal, diurnal; rests for several hours during the day, especially if it is hot, in a sheltered spot such as under a fallen log, beneath a shrub or in a rock crevice

Tracks: forepaw and hind paw 1½-1¾" (4-4.5 cm), round, heel pad smooth, toes evenly spread, lacking claw marks; straight line of tracks; hind paws fall close to or onto the fore prints (direct register) when walking, often obliterating forepaw tracks, 6-9" (15-23 cm) stride

Stan's Notes: A small cat with a unique shape, having a flattened, elongated head and shorter front legs than hind legs, making it look as though it is perpetually going downhill. Not well studied, so solid biological information is in short supply.

Very secretive, with a range from South and Central America into southern Arizona and the tip of southern Texas. There are no known breeding populations north of Mexico, but occasionally one jaguarundi is seen. It is possible that some of these are the offspring of feral house cats. There are also reports of captive jaguarundi escaping and living in the wild.

Apparently doesn't mind water and occasionally swims to cross rivers. Solitary throughout most of the year, with males seeking females for mating.

One of the few cat species in which offspring of the same litter can be different color morphs. Kittens are born with light spots, which soon fade with age.

Bobcat
Lynx rufus

Family: Cats (Felidae)

Size: L 2¼-3½' (69-107 cm); T 3-7" (7.5-18 cm); H 18-24" (45-61 cm)

Weight: 14-30 lb. (6.3-13.5 kg)

Description: Tawny brown during summer. Light gray during winter with dark streaks and spots. Long stiff fur projects down from jowls and tapers to a point (cheek ruffs). Triangular ears, tipped with short black hairs (tufts). Prominent white spot on the back of ears. Dark horizontal barring on upper legs. Short stubby tail with a black tip on the top and sides and a white underside. Male slightly larger than female.

Origin/Age: native; 10-15 years

Compare: Much smaller than the Mountain Lion (pg. 303), which has a long rope-like tail. Ocelot (pg. 291) and Jaguarundi (pg. 295) are smaller and not regularly seen in Arizona. Look for ear tufts and a white underside of tail to help identify Bobcat.

Habitat: mixed forests, fields, farmlands, elevations up to 12,000' (3,660 m)

Home: den, often in a hollow log, rock crevice or under a pile of tree branches filled with leaves

Food: carnivore; medium to small mammals such as rabbits and mice; also eats birds and carrion

Sounds: raspy meows and yelps, purrs when content

Breeding: Feb-Mar mating; 60-70 days gestation

Young: 1-7 (usually 3) kittens once per year in April or May

scat

Signs: scratching posts with claw marks 3-4' (.9-1.2 m) aboveground, caches of larger kills covered with a light layer of leaves and twigs, scent posts marked with urine; long cylindrical scat, contains hair and bones, often buried, sometimes visible beneath a thin layer of dirt and debris

Activity: nocturnal, diurnal; often rests on hot days in a sheltered spot such as under a fallen log or in a rock crevice

Tracks: forepaw and hind paw 2" (5 cm), round, multi-lobed heel pad, 4 toes on all feet, lacking claw marks; straight line of tracks; hind paws fall near or on fore prints (direct register) when walking, often obliterating forepaw tracks, 9-13" (23-33 cm) stride

Stan's Notes: This is the most common wildcat species in Arizona. Much more common than all the cats found in the state, thriving in nearly all habitat types. The common name refers to the short, stubby or "bobbed" tail. Frequently walks with tail curled upward, which exposes the white underside, making this animal easy to identify. Makes sounds similar to a house cat.

Often uses the same trails in its territory to patrol for rabbits, which is its favorite food, and other prey. Does not climb trees as much as the Mountain Lion (pg. 303), but swims well. Hunts by stalking or laying in wait to attack (ambushing). Ambushes prey by rushing forward, chases and captures it, then kills it with a bite to the neck. Has been known to go without eating for several weeks during periods of famine.

Male has a larger territory than female. Usually solitary except for mating and when mothers are with young. Male will seek out a female in heat. Several males may follow a female until she is ready for mating.

Female does not breed until her second year. She has a primary (natal) den in which kittens are born and live for a short time after birth. Female also has secondary dens in her territory, where she may move her young if the natal den is disturbed. Dens are used only by the females and young. Mother raises young on her own.

kittens

Kittens are born well furred and with spots. Their eyes are closed at birth and open at about 10 days. They are weaned at approximately 8 weeks, when they start to hunt with their mother. Young stay with their mother until about 7 months, when she disperses them to mate.

Mountain Lion
Puma concolor

Family: Cats (Felidae)

Size: L 5-6' (1.5-1.8 m); T 24-36" (61-91 cm); H 30-36" (76-91 cm)

Weight: M 80-267 lb. (36-120 kg); F 64-142 lb. (29-64 kg)

Description: Overall light to tawny brown with light gray-to-white underside. White upper lip and chin, pink nose, dark spot at base of white whiskers. Small oval ears. Long legs. Large round feet. Long rope-like tail with a dark tip.

Origin/Age: native; 10-20 years

Compare: Bobcat (pg. 299) is much smaller, with a short tail. The Jaguar (pg. 307) is slightly larger and covered with spots. Look for a long rope-like tail to identify the Mountain Lion.

Habitat: river valleys, woodlands, unpopulated locations above 7,000' (2,135 m) in elevation

Home: den, often a sheltered rock crevice, thicket, cave or other protected place; female uses den only to give birth, male does not use den

Food: carnivore; larger mammals such as hares, rabbits, opossums, raccoons, javelinas, skunks and deer

Sounds: purrs when content or with cubs, growls, snarls and hisses when threatened or in defense, loud frightening scream during mating, rarely roars

Breeding: year-round mating; 90-100 days gestation

Young: 1-6 (usually 3) cubs once every 2 years; born helpless and blind, covered with dark spots until 3 months, leaves den at 40-70 days and does not return, remains with mother until 15 months

stalking

cubs

scat

Signs: long scratches and gashes above 5' (1.5 m) on larger tree trunks, small piles of urine-soaked dirt and debris (serving as scent posts), caches of uneaten prey covered with small branches and leaves; large cylindrical scat up to 10" (25 cm) long and 2" (5 cm) wide, contains hair and bones, sometimes lightly covered with dirt

Activity: primarily nocturnal, to a lesser extent crepuscular; active all year, usually rests in a tree in daytime, rests near a recent kill

Tracks: forepaw and hind paw 5-6" (13-15 cm), round, lobed heel pad, toes evenly spread, lacks claw marks; straight line of tracks; hind paws fall near or onto fore prints (direct register) when walking, often obliterating forepaw tracks, 12-28" (30-71 cm) stride

Stan's Notes: The Mountain Lion was the most widely ranging cat in the New World in the early 1800s, from Canada to the tip of South America. It was hunted by government professionals to protect livestock from attack until the 1960s. Now seen only in scattered places throughout Arizona, often in remote unpopulated areas. Usually secretive and avoids humans, but has been known to attack people.

Contrary to the popular belief that it harms the deer population, it usually hunts and kills only about once each week, feeding for many days on the same kill. It hunts by stalking and springing from cover or dropping from a tree. Frequently drags its kill to a secluded area to eat, buries the carcass and returns to feed over the next couple days, often at night. It is an excellent climber and can leap distances up to 20 feet (6.1 m). Will swim if necessary.

Some people mistakenly think this cat will make a good pet and do not know what to do when their "pet" starts to knock down family members and bite them. These "pets" are released and then often turn up in suburban areas. Usually these are the animals that attack people since they have lost their fear of humans.

Home range of the male is 54-115 square miles (140-299 sq. km) and excludes other male mountain lions. Female range is nearly half the size of the male territory.

Solitary animal except for mating. During that time, the male accompanies the female for up to a couple weeks, traveling and sleeping with her. The female matures sexually at 2-3 years. Only the female raises the young.

RARE

Jaguar
Panthera onca

Family: Cats (Felidae)

Size: L 5-6¼' (1.5-1.9 m); T 17-27" (43-69 cm); H 28-34" (71-86 cm)

Weight: 75-325 lb. (34-146 kg)

Description: Overall tan to yellow and covered in black spots or rings in horizontal rows. Rings have 1-2 small spots inside. A large head with short round ears. Short stout legs. Long, thick rope-like tail with black spots and rings. Legs, head and tail have solid spots. Rarely entirely black with faint spots. Male slightly larger than female.

Origin/Age: native; 10-20 years

Compare: Mountain Lion (pg. 303) adult is slightly smaller and lacks spots; young lions just have faint spotting. Much larger than Ocelot (pg. 291), which appears more like a house cat and isn't regularly found in Arizona.

Habitat: mixed forests, fields, farmlands, elevations up to 12,000' (3,660 m)

Home: den for giving birth, often in a hollow log, rock crevice or beneath a pile of tree branches filled with leaves

Food: carnivore; medium to large mammals such as rabbits, deer, coatis, javelinas

Sounds: roars, snarls

Breeding: Dec-Jan mating; 93-110 days gestation

Young: 2-4 kittens once per year in April or May; born blind, leaves the den after 3 weeks, can remain with the mother for up to 2 years

307

Signs: caches of larger kills covered with a light layer of leaves and twigs, scent posts marked with urine (often seen only during winter when urine sprays onto snow); large cylindrical scat up to 10" (25 cm) long and 2" (5 cm) wide, contains hair and bones, sometimes lightly covered with dirt

Activity: nocturnal; rests during the day in a sheltered spot such as under a fallen log or in a rock crevice

Tracks: forepaw 4-4½" (10-11 cm), hind paw 5-6½" (13-16 cm), round, lobed heel pad, toes evenly spread, lacks claw marks; straight line of tracks; hind paws fall near or on the fore prints (direct register) when walking, often obliterating the forepaw tracks, 12-28" (30-71 cm) stride

Stan's Notes: This is the largest and most powerful cat in North, Central and South America. Third largest cat in the world behind the African lion and tiger. Rare in Arizona. Ranges to Patagonia, South America, and wanders over a very large area, with some jaguars covering 200 square miles (520 sq. km). Always on the move in search of food. Hunts mainly on the ground by stalking and pouncing mostly on large prey such as deer and javelinas.

Where its common name comes from is unclear. South American Indians reportedly call it a fierce dog or large-bodied dog. Its jaws are more powerful than those of the Mountain Lion (pg. 303), enabling it to feed on very large animals and even to bite through their skulls.

A good climber, but does not spend as much time in trees as the Mountain Lion. Unlike other cats, it loves water and is a good swimmer, often resting while half submerged. Solitary except for the breeding season, when males seek females. With such large territories and so few individuals, many do not breed every year. Reports of males staying with females and even bringing food to the young for the first year are not substantiated.

Young stay with their mother and start to hunt at age 6 months; some individuals stay with the mother for up to 24 months. The young are dispersed by the mother when she is ready to breed again. Young become sexually mature at 3 years of age.

Revered by many native peoples. The Mayans believed it to be the god of the underworld, helping the sun to travel underneath the earth at night, ensuring it would rise each morning.

All-black jaguars (melanistic) occur, but they are uncommon and may be found only in dark jungle habitats in the wild. In some individuals spots are sometimes still visible. These individuals are known as Black Panthers, but they are not a separate species. Any of these animals seen in Arizona are probably the result of escape.

Javelina
Pecari tajacu

Family: Peccaries (Tayassuidae)

Size: L 3-4' (.9-1.2); T 1-2" (2.5-5 cm); H 20-24" (50-61 cm)

Weight: 30-60 lb. (13.5-27 kg)

Description: Large thick body and short dark legs. Dark brown to nearly black with a grizzled appearance. Faint, narrow white collar from shoulder to shoulder. Flexible cartilaginous snout like that of domestic pigs. Tiny dark eyes. Small well-furred ears. Very small straight tail, hard to see, not curled like domestic pigs. Straight tusks, 1-2" (2.5-5 cm) long, showing just the tips at the sides of mouth.

Origin/Age: native; 15-20 years

Compare: Domesticated pigs have a coiled tail and do not have dark fur. Feral pigs are much larger, with a less uniform color and tusks pointing upward.

Habitat: open forests, shrublands, semideserts, elevations below 6,000' (1,830 m)

Home: no den or nest; constantly on the move but never too far from water, rests in the open or under a tree, seeking shelter from the heat

Food: herbivore; prickly pear cacti, mesquite fruit, stool and agave plants, roots and tubers

Sounds: snorts and grunts, squeals, barking alarm call

Breeding: any time of year; 21 weeks gestation

Young: 1-3 reds once per year; remains red with a dark stripe down the back for up to 3 months, nurses for 3 months, nursing from behind the mother's hind legs while she stands

red

tusks

young fighting

Signs: chewed cacti, especially prickly pear, a strong musky odor, large holes in the ground where it has uprooted plants, mud holes for wallowing; large irregular scat segments or large, flattened round patties

scat

Activity: all times; feeds every several hours in winter, resting in between; takes a longer break during the heat of the day in summer, sleeping in the shade of a shrub or tree

Tracks: front hoof ¾-1½" (2-4 cm) long, cloven, pointed in the front, hind hoof slightly smaller; offset line of paired tracks; hind hooves fall near fore prints (no direct register) when walking

Stan's Notes: The javelina (pronounced "HA-veh-LEE-nah") is the only native pig-like animal found in North America. It occurs throughout the American tropics up through Mexico and into the southern half of Arizona, parts of New Mexico and western and southern Texas.

Wild and domestic pigs came from Europe (Old World) and are only distantly related to javelinas. The javelina has a scent gland on its back above the tail that gives the animal a characteristic smell; pigs do not have this. Javelina tusks are short and straight, pointing down, while pig tusks are curved and point upward. Javelina tails are short, furred and straight; hog tails are long, naked and curly. The javelina usually has only 2 offspring at a time, but a pig has up to 20 at one time. Unlike pigs, javelinas are highly social, forming permanent herds with cooperation among the members.

Herds consist of as many as 50 individuals, but smaller groups are more common. Will all lay side by side to help keep warm on cold nights. A dominant male leads the pack and performs all the mating. Young (reds) are protected by the entire herd. Parents break up fights between youngsters.

Has very poor vision, but an excellent sense of smell. Also called Musk Hog due to the scent gland. Each herd has its own unique smell that helps individuals identify other members of the herd. New members are born into the pack and remain for their entire lives. Strangers are rarely taken in.

When a javelina is alarmed, the dark mane stands erect. Always on the move in search of food. Never far from water because it needs to drink often. Usually shy and secretive, but can be tame in suburban areas.

male

Pronghorn
Antilocapra americana

Family: Pronghorn (Antilocapridae)

Size: L 4-4½' (1.2-1.4 m); T 3-7" (7.5-18 cm); H 3-3½' (.9-1.1 m)

Weight: M 100-140 lb. (45-63 kg); F 75-100 lb. (34-45 kg)

Description: Neck, back and outer legs are light tan to reddish tan. White patches on chin, neck, chest, sides and rump. Ears are trimmed in black. Male horns are 12-20" (30-50 cm) long, black, each with a single point curving inward and small tine about halfway up. Female horns are 3-4" (7.5-10 cm) long, black, each with 1 point and lacking a tine.

Origin/Age: native; 5-10 years

Compare: White-tailed Deer (pg. 319) lacks the white sides and black horns of the Pronghorn.

Habitat: scrublands, grasslands, farmlands, ranches, semi-deserts, elevations below 6,000' (1,830 m)

Home: no den or nest; rests in open terrain, does not seek shelter to give birth or escape bad weather

Food: herbivore; grasses and other green plants

Sounds: usually quiet, snorts loudly to show aggression toward another Pronghorn

Breeding: Sep-Oct mating; 7-8 months gestation; implantation delayed until 1 month after mating

Young: 2 offspring once per year in May or June; 3-13 lb. (1.4-5.9 kg), can walk within minutes of birth, grayer than adult, acquires adult coloration at about 1 month

315

female

scat

Signs: oval depressions in snow or leaves are evidence of beds; scat in groups of small oval pellets when it has eaten woody material, masses of large segmented scat when it has fed on green plants

Activity: diurnal, nocturnal; often seen grazing in large open fields, grasslands and scrublands

Tracks: front hoof 3" (7.5 cm) long, hind hoof slightly smaller, both with a split heart shape with the point in the front; neat line of single tracks; hind hooves fall near or directly onto fore prints (direct register) when walking, often obliterating the front hoof tracks, heart shape widens when walking in mud or running

Stan's Notes: The fastest land animal in North America. Achieves speeds of up to 70 mph (113 km/h) for short distances, with a cruising speed of 30-40 mph (48-64 km/h). Will simply outrun a predator such as a wolf. Can leap approximately 20 feet (6.1 m) horizontally while running, but is reluctant to jump a standard-height barbed wire fence, choosing to crawl underneath it or pass through between the strands.

Also known as the American Antelope, even though it is not an antelope. The common name "Pronghorn" comes from the small tine or prong located halfway up the horns of the male (buck). It has true horns, which are made of hair-like (keratin) sheaths over bony cores, as opposed to antlers. The only horned animal that sheds horns. Horns are shed annually, usually in November or December after the rut. Shed horns break down quickly in the environment and are rarely found. About one-third of females (does) lack horns; the rest have small horns.

Eyesight is said to be eight times better than human sight. Able to spot predators approaching from long distances. Well suited to life on the open range, with herds traveling great distances to find good grazing areas. Can tolerate cold, but not deep snow.

The buck will gather a harem and start to defend territory during March. If trapped, a buck will fall back behind the herd and fight off the predator with its horns and by kicking.

The doe becomes sexually mature at 16 months. A doe usually produces only one offspring per year for the first couple of years, while an older female will often have twins or sometimes triplets.

Babies spend their first week or so hiding in tall grass, with their mother returning regularly to nurse. The young can outrun most predators at about 1 week of age.

male

White-tailed Deer
Odocoileus virginianus couesi

Family: Deer (Cervidae)

Size: L 3-6' (.9-1.8 m); T 6-12" (15-30 cm); H 3-4' (.9-1.2 m)

Weight: M 70-120 lb. (32-54 kg); F 50-75 lb. (23-34 kg)

Description: Reddish brown during summer, grayish brown during winter. Large ears, white inside with black edges. A white eye-ring, nose band, chin, throat and belly. Brown tail with a black tip and white underside. Male has antlers with many tines and an antler spread of 12-36" (30-91 cm). Female has a thinner neck than male and lacks antlers.

Origin/Age: native; 5-10 years

Compare: Smaller and less common than the Mule Deer (pg. 323), which has a small, thin white tail with a black tip. Elk (pg. 327) has a dark mane and is much larger and heavier than White-tailed Deer.

Habitat: all habitats, all elevations

Home: no den or nest; sleeps in a different spot every night, beds may be concentrated in one area, does not use a shelter in bad weather or winter, will move to a semisheltered area (yard) with a good supply of food in winter

Food: herbivore; grasses and other green plants, acorns and nuts in summer, twigs and buds in winter

Sounds: loud whistle-like snorts, male grunts, fawn bleats

Breeding: late Oct-Nov mating; 6-7 months gestation

Young: 1-2 fawns once per year in May or June; covered with white spots, walks within hours of birth

young male

tree rub

Coues female

scat

Signs: browsed twigs that are ripped or torn (due to the lack of upper incisor teeth), tree rubs (saplings scraped or stripped of bark) made by male while polishing antlers during the rut, oval depressions in grass or leaves are evidence of beds; round, hard brown pellets during winter, segmented cylindrical masses of scat in spring and summer

Activity: nocturnal, crepuscular; often moves along same trails to visit feeding areas

Tracks: front hoof 2-3" (5-7.5 cm) long, hind hoof slightly smaller, both with a split heart shape with the point in the front; neat line of single tracks; hind hooves fall near or directly onto fore prints (direct register) when walking

Stan's Notes: Almost extirpated in the 1920s. It has recovered well and is now found in most river bottoms in southeastern Arizona. In Arizona the White-tailed Deer is actually a subspecies

fawn

known as Coues White-tailed Deer. Coues Whitetails look the same as White-tailed Deer (*O. virginianus*), their eastern counterpart, except that they are smaller and weigh less. Also called Virginia Deer or just Whitetail.

Much longer guard hairs in winter give the animal a larger appearance than in summer. Individual hairs of the winter coat are thick and hollow and provide excellent insulation.

In summer, antlers are covered with a furry skin called velvet. Velvet contains a network of blood vessels that supplies nutrients to the growing antlers. New antler growth begins after the male (buck) drops his antlers in January or February. Some females (does) have been known to grow antlers.

Deer are dependent on the location of the food supply. In winter large groups move to low moist areas (yards) that have plenty of food. Yarding behavior provides some protection from predators. Eats 5-9 pounds (2.3-4.1 kg) of food per day, preferring acorns in fall and fresh grass in spring. Its four-chambered stomach enables the animal to get nutrients from poor food sources, such as twigs, and eat and drink substances that are unsuitable for people.

Able to run up to 37 mph (60 km/h), jump up to 8½ feet (2.6 m) high and leap 30 feet (9.1 m). Also an excellent swimmer.

The buck is solitary in spring and early summer, but seeks other bucks in late summer and early fall to spar. Bucks are polygamous. The largest, most dominant bucks mate with many does.

For a couple weeks after birth, fawns lay still all day while their mother is away feeding. Mother nurses them evenings and nights.

male

Mule Deer
Odocoileus hemionus

Family: Deer (Cervidae)

Size: L 4-7½' (1.2-2.3 m); T 4-9" (10-23 cm); H 3½-4' (1.1-1.2 m)

Weight: M 100-250 lb. (45-113 kg); F 75-150 lb. (34-68 kg)

Description: Reddish brown in summer. Gray in winter. White chin, throat and rump. Large ears, white inside with black tips and edges. A thin white tail with a black tip. Male has large antlers with 2 main beams, many tines and an antler spread of 2-4' (61-122 cm). Female is 20 percent smaller than male, has a thinner neck and lacks antlers.

Origin/Age: native; 10-15 years

Compare: Larger, stockier and more common than White-tailed Deer (pg. 319), which has a larger, wider tail. Antlers on White-tailed Deer have just 1 main beam. Mule Deer runs with its tail down, while the White-tailed Deer runs with its tail raised and waving back and forth.

Habitat: grasslands, semideserts, scrublands, forests, all elevations

Home: no den or nest; doesn't use shelter in bad weather or winter, sleeps in dense cover each night

Food: herbivore; grasses and other green plants, acorns and nuts in summer, twigs and buds in winter

Sounds: generally quiet, male will grunt, fawn will bleat when it calls to its mother

Breeding: late Nov-Dec mating; 6-7 months gestation

Young: 1-2 fawns once per year in May or June; covered with white spots, walks within hours of birth

young male

fawn

female

scat

Signs: ripped or torn browsed twigs (due to the lack of upper incisor teeth), oval depressions in grass or leaves are evidence of beds; segmented cylindrical masses of scat in spring and summer, round, hard brown pellets during winter

Activity: nocturnal, crepuscular; will wander about seeking feeding areas with grass

Tracks: front hoof 2½-3¼" (6-8 cm) long, hind hoof slightly smaller, both with a split heart shape with the point in the front; neat line of single tracks; hind hooves fall near or directly onto fore prints (direct register) when walking, fore hooves fall in front of hind prints when bounding in a distinctive gait (stotting)

Stan's Notes: The largest of the two deer species in Arizona. Over the past 100-150 years, Mule Deer populations have risen and fallen dramatically from times of few individuals and near extinction to years of overpopulation. Population seems stable now. A common resident across most of Arizona in nearly all ecosystems.

Also called Black-tailed Deer for its black-tipped tail. Common name "Mule" comes from its large mule-like ears, which can move independently to focus on sounds originating from two different directions simultaneously. Although the ears appear substantially larger than those of White-tailed Deer (pg. 319), measurements confirm that they are about the same in both species.

Mule Deer have a unique, stiff-legged bounding gait called stotting, in which the front and hind legs move in the same fashion at the same time. Stotting helps to positively identify this animal since White-tailed Deer do not do this.

The male (buck) drops its antlers in January or February, with new growth beginning immediately. Growing antlers are covered with a velvety covering that contains a network of blood vessels. Each successive set of antlers gets larger until a buck reaches peak maturity at 6-7 years. Antlers grown after that age range have an irregular growth pattern, resulting in atypically shaped antlers. Antler growth is also affected by the amount and quality of food available. Bucks are solitary until just before the rut, when several may come together to look for females (does). Sparring between bucks is common. The objective is to overpower the opponent, and injury rarely results. Highly polygamous, a dominant buck will mate with nearly all does in his area.

Does remain in small to large groups year-round. A doe may mate with more than one buck per season. Younger does will produce single fawns, while older does produce twins annually. Fawns remain hidden in tall vegetation for their first month. Mothers visit their young each evening to nurse.

male

Elk
Cervus elaphus

Family: Deer (Cervidae)

Size: L 7-9½' (2.1-2.9 m); T 3-8" (7.5-20 cm); H 4½-5' (1.4-1.5 m)

Weight: M 600-1,100 lb. (270-495 kg); F 450-650 lb. (203-293 kg)

Description: Brown to tan with a darker head, neck, belly and legs. Rump patch is light tan to yellowish. Short stubby tail. Male has large antlers with many tines and an antler spread of 4-5' (1.2-1.5 m). Female has a lighter mane than male, a thinner neck and lacks antlers.

Origin/Age: native; 15-20 years

Compare: Elk is much larger and heavier than its cousin, the White-tailed Deer (pg. 319), which lacks the dark mane.

Habitat: mixed forests, fields, grasslands, elevations above 6,000' (1,830 m)

Home: no den or nest; rests out in the open on the ground, will bed in a different area each night

Food: herbivore; grasses and other green plants

Sounds: snorts and grunts, male gives a bugle call or high-pitched whistle to challenge other males during rut; call can be heard up to several miles away

Breeding: late Aug-Nov mating; 9 months gestation

Young: 1-2 calves once per year in June or July; covered with spots until about 3 months, feeds solely by nursing for the first 30 days, weaned at 9 months

bugling

sparring

female

summer scat

winter scat

Signs: tree rubs (saplings scraped or stripped of bark) made by the male while polishing antlers during rut, ground scrapes (shallow depressions in the ground) made by male hooves to attract females and where male urinates and defecates, shallow depressions in grass made from resting

Activity: nocturnal, crepuscular; can be seen during the day walking and feeding

Tracks: front hoof 4-4½" (10-11 cm) long, hind hoof slightly smaller, both with a split heart shape with the point in the front; line of individual tracks; hind hooves fall near or onto fore prints (direct register) when walking, often obliterating the front hoof tracks; heart shape widens and 2 dots (made by dewclaws) print just behind each heart-shaped print when in mud

Stan's Notes: There is only one species of elk in North America, but there are four subspecies. Sometimes called Wapiti, which is a Shawnee Indian word meaning "pale deer." The British name for the moose is "Elk." This name apparently was misapplied by our early settlers and has remained since.

Once widespread in the western United States, with numbers at about 10 million before European settlement. Almost disappeared, dwindling down to 500-600 individuals by the early 1900s due to overhunting, and extirpated from Arizona. All elk seen in the state now are the result of reintroduction. In 1913, 83 individuals were transplanted from Yellowstone National Park to begin an Arizona elk herd. Today there are more than 35,000 elk in the state.

A highly gregarious animal. Most herds consist of many females (cows) and calves. Highly territorial, marking the edges of its area with a scent secreted from glands on the sides of its chin and muzzle. Makes a shallow, saucer-like depression in dirt (wallow) in which it rolls, coating its fur with dust to help protect against annoying insects. It is a fast animal, with males (bulls) capable of reaching 35 mph (56 km/h) for short distances. Also a strong swimmer that will wade across nearly any river or stream.

A bull is solitary or found in small groups, but will join the herd during the rut. Bulls are capable of breeding at 2 years. However, rarely is a bull large enough at that age to fight off older males and establish a harem. Will thrash small trees to polish its antlers. Tears up vegetation and wears it on antlers to express dominance. Top bulls challenge each other by clashing their antlers together in a jousting fashion. Rarely do these fights result in any injury or death. The most polygamous animal in America, one bull will mate with all cows in the harem.

The cow becomes sexually mature at 3 years. A cow will leave the herd to give birth, rejoining the group 4-10 days later.

Burro
Equus asinus

Family: Horses (Equidae)

Size: L 4-5' (1.2-1.5 m); T 12-24" (30-61 cm); H 4-4½' (1.2-1.4 m)

Weight: 400-650 lb. (180-293 kg)

Description: Wide variety of colors and patterns, but all have the same general size and shape of a small horse with large ears. May have faint zebra-like striping on the sides. Long snout, often white. Short erect mane, black-tipped tail and stout legs. Dark stripe from mane to tail and across shoulders.

Origin/Age: non-native; 20-35 years

Compare: Smaller than horses. Look for the large ears, large head, short erect mane and slow calm nature. No branding or other marks. Found in the deserts alone or in small groups in remote wild areas and on public lands.

Habitat: semideserts, deserts, shrublands, valleys, below 7,500' (2,285 m)

Home: no den or nest; rests in open terrain, does not seek shelter to give birth or escape bad weather

Food: herbivore; grasses and other green plants, small thin twigs

Sounds: typical donkey heehaws, squeals and snorts

Breeding: any time of year; 12 months (360-370 days) gestation; female becomes sexually mature at 2 years

Young: 1 foal once per year; weighs 20-30 pounds (9-13.5 kg) at birth, able to walk within 30 minutes, nurses for 4-5 months

Signs: oval depressions in snow or grass are evidence of beds; scat in piles of large patties, large amounts of urine, sometimes pooling on flat open ground

Activity: diurnal; feeds for up to several hours before resting for up to 2 hours and feeding again, may take a break at midday

Tracks: front and hind hooves 2-3" (5-7.5 cm) wide, each a large single semicircle; wide space between each print; hind hooves do not register in fore prints

Stan's Notes: A non-native species originally from northern Africa and the Arabian peninsula that was introduced around the world. Rare in Arizona. Occurs in deserts and semideserts in small groups consisting of one male, two females and their young. Herds often break up and reform. Dominant males, usually 3-5 years of age, sometimes defend territories and often tolerate subordinate males.

Also called Donkey, Wild Donkey or Wild Ass. Closely related to horses and interbreeds with them, producing hybrids. Burros breeding with horses and zebras produce hybrids that cannot reproduce (sterile). A cross between a male burro (jack) and a female horse produces a mule. A cross between a female burro (jenny) and a male horse produces a hinny. A cross between a burro and a zebra produces a zebra or what is known as a zonkey.

Very important to civilizations around the world, playing a role in human economies from the time of the ancient Egyptians to the present. Has been domesticated as a pack animal for about 6,000 years. Capable of carrying more than 200 pounds (30 kg) for extended periods of time. Known to go without food and water for several days.

Most active in early morning and late in the afternoon, when it feeds on grasses. Often rests during midday. Will sleep standing up or laying down. Has excellent vision, keen hearing and a good sense of smell.

Burros are very observant and cautious animals that will refuse to do anything out of the ordinary or dangerous. This behavior has given them the reputation of being stubborn as a mule. However, most burros that have been domesticated are quite passive and make wonderful companions for both people and horses.

Feral Horse
Equus caballus

Family: Horses (Equidae)

Size: L 5-7' (1.5-2.1 m); T 12-24" (30-61 cm); H 4½-5½' (1.4-1.7 m)

Weight: M 800-900 lb. (360-405 kg); F 550-750 lb. (248-338 kg)

Description: Nearly identical to domestic horses in size, shape and color, with many colors and patterns. Large powerful body. Long snout. Long mane and tail. May have faint zebra-like striping on the sides.

Origin/Age: non-native; 20-35 years

Compare: Slightly smaller than domestic horses, otherwise extremely hard to differentiate from afar except for its behavior. The Feral Horse is often skittish, scruffy-looking and has no branding. Look for it in large, remote wild areas and public lands.

Habitat: semideserts, shrublands, valleys, elevations up to 7,500' (2,285 m)

Home: no den or nest; rests in open terrain, does not seek shelter to give birth or escape bad weather

Food: herbivore; grasses and other green plants, shrubs and other woody plants

Sounds: typical horse whinnies, nickers, squeals, neighs and snorts

Breeding: Jun-Aug mating; 11 months gestation

Young: 1 colt once every other year in May or June; can walk within minutes of birth, nurses for several weeks

flehmening

mother and colt

Signs: oval depressions in snow or grass are evidence of beds; scat in piles of large patties, several males will use a common defecation site, resulting in a large formation called a stud pile; large amounts of urine, sometimes pooling on flat open ground

Activity: diurnal; feeds for up to several hours, rests for up to 2 hours, then feeds again, may take a break at midday

Tracks: front and hind hooves 3-5" (7.5-13 cm) wide, each a large single semicircle; wide space between each print; hind hooves do not register in fore prints

Stan's Notes: Horses were domesticated over 5,000 years ago in the Old World and have been introduced all over the world. The Feral Horse, sometimes known as Wild Horse, has a wide variety of colors and patterns. While often a bit smaller than domestic horses, from a distance it is nearly impossible to differentiate wild and domestic horses from each other when they are grazing on public lands. In Arizona, however, the Feral Horse is rare.

Diet is 90 percent grass, so the Feral won't be seen far from open grass habitat. Also needs to be near freestanding water. Typically visits a local watering hole at least daily, often in late afternoon.

Social structure is complex. Usually seen in small herds of mostly adult females (mares), their young (colts) and a dominant male (stallion). Individuals seen on their own are usually injured or young stallions who have yet to establish themselves in a herd.

Young stallions are forced out of their herds at age 3 and form small bachelor herds, led by a dominant stallion. Fights between stallions start with threat postures and displays such as laying the ears back, opening the mouth, arching the neck and shaking the head. Physical fights include biting and kicking, often resulting in serious injury.

Takes a dust bath by rolling in exposed soils. Mutual grooming is a daily activity, although a stallion does not groom or allow itself to be groomed.

male

Desert Bighorn Sheep
Ovis canadensis nelsoni

Family: Goats, Sheep and Cattle (Bovidae)

Size: L 4-6' (1.2-1.8 m); T 3-6" (7.5-15 cm); H 2½-3½' (76-107 cm)

Weight: M 150-225 lb. (68-101 kg); F 75-130 lb. (34-59 kg)

Description: Stocky and muscular, with a thick neck. Overall light tan to brown with a white rump. Short dark tail. White-tipped muzzle. Extremely large horns, curled, heavily ridged, pointing forward. Female is overall tan to brown with a thin neck, short legs, short oval ears and short, backward curving horns. Coloring of both sexes varies seasonally.

Origin/Age: native; 10-15 years

Compare: Look for the large, distinctive curled horns of the male or the short tan-colored horns of the female to help identify the Desert Bighorn Sheep.

Habitat: mountains, rocky cliffs, coniferous and deciduous forests, valleys, elevations above 7,500' (2,285 m)

Home: no den or nest; rests in open terrain, does not seek shelter to give birth or escape bad weather

Food: herbivore; grasses and other green plants, shrubs and other woody plants

Sounds: usually quiet

Breeding: Nov-Dec mating; 6 months gestation

Young: 1 lamb once per year in May or June; can walk within minutes of birth, nurses for several weeks, eats forage at 2 weeks, weaned at 5-6 months

ewes and lambs

female

scat

Signs: oval depressions in grass are evidence of beds; scat in single round pellets when it has consumed dried woody plants, masses of large segmented scat when it has fed on green plants

Activity: diurnal; feeds for up to several hours, sits down to rest for up to 2 hours, then feeds again

Tracks: front hoof 2½-3" (6-7.5 cm) long, hind hoof slightly smaller, widely split at the front with a point in the front; neat line of single tracks; hind hooves fall near or directly onto fore prints (direct register) when walking, often obliterating the front hoof tracks, widens when walking in mud or running

Stan's Notes: This magnificent mammal exemplifies the Rocky Mountains, but can be found in a wide variety of locations and habitats. While often thought of as an animal of high mountains and steep canyons, evidence shows that this may be a function imposed by people from hunting pressures. Historically it ranged out into the foothills and eastern plains in Arizona.

Also called Mountain Sheep or Bighorns. The Desert Bighorn in Arizona is actually a smaller, thinner subspecies of Bighorn Sheep (*O. canadensis*), with the horns of the adult Desert Bighorn male (ram) curving back and spreading away from the head more than is seen in male Bighorn Sheep. Massive, heavily ridged horns can be useful in determining the age of a ram. Horns sweeping back and outward, then forward and curving upward eventually form what is called a full curl. Horn tips are often torn or broken, a condition known as brooming. Rams with full curl horns are 7-8 years of age. Horns of younger rams are shorter and more slender.

A gregarious and social animal, with females (ewes) and young (lambs) forming large herds that travel, feed and play together. Older rams form small bachelor herds.

Rams don't breed until 7-8 years of age, when they have full curl horns, with horn size determining the breeding status. The most dominant ram will do most of the breeding of the ewe herd. Ewes breed at 2-3 years of age.

Rams are well known for butting their heads during the rut. They will charge each other at speeds up to 20 mph (32 km/h), crashing their bony foreheads together, resulting in a very loud crack that can be heard from more than a mile away.

Hooves have a hard bony edge and soft spongy center, allowing the animal to scamper over rocky surfaces with ease. Makes short, seasonal migrations from summer to winter ranges.

male

RARE

American Bison
Bison bison

Family: Goats, Sheep and Cattle (Bovidae)

Size: L 8-12' (2.4-3.7 m); T 12-19" (30-48 cm); H 5-6' (1-5-1.8 m)

Weight: M 1,000-2,000 lb. (450-900 kg); F 800-1,000 lb. (360-450 kg)

Description: Dark brown head, lighter brown body and large humped shoulders. Bearded with a long shaggy mane over head and shoulders. Long tuft-tipped tail. Both sexes have short curved horns, which are not shed.

Origin/Age: native; 20-25 years

Compare: A massive animal, hard to confuse with any other. No longer roams freely in Arizona. Rarely seen beyond established, managed areas.

Habitat: scrublands, semideserts, open forests, mountains, elevations below 10,000' (3,050 m)

Home: does not use a den or nest, even in bad weather or winter; beds in a different spot each night, rests in the open, laying on the ground

Food: herbivore; grasses and other green plants, lichens

Sounds: often quiet; male bellows during the rut, female snorts, young bawls for mother's attention

Breeding: Jul-Aug mating; 9-10 months gestation

Young: 1 calf every 1-2 years in May or June; born with reddish brown fur, stands within 30 minutes, walks within hours of its birth, joins herd at 2-3 days, acquires hump, horns and adult coloration at 2-3 months, weaned at 6-7 months

flehmening   female

scat

Signs: saucer-like depressions in dirt (wallows), 8-10' (2.4-3 m) wide, trees and shrubs with the bark rubbed off, shallow depressions in the grass are evidence of bison beds; scat is similar to that of the domestic cow, flat round patties, 12-14" (30-36 cm) wide

Activity: crepuscular; often rests during the day to chew its cud

Tracks: front hoof 6-7" (15-18 cm) long, hind hoof slightly smaller, both with opposing crescents and more pointed in the front; hind hooves fall behind and slightly to the side of fore prints; crescents widen when walking in mud or running

Stan's Notes: The largest land mammal in North America and considered unique to the New World. Sometimes called Buffalo, but not related to the Old World buffalo. Historically it ranged across most of the United States, at one time numbering in the tens of millions. Hunted to near extinction around 1830, when a government policy advocated extermination. By the early 1900s fewer than 1,000 bison remained in America.

It is thought that bison didn't occur in Arizona prior to European settlement, but it is possible since herds are nomadic. All bison now in Arizona are a result of introductions starting in the early 1900s and the 1940s and 1950s. The few herds in Arizona are found only on wildlife management areas and private ranches.

Centuries ago, great herds would migrate long distances between winter and summer grounds. While seen in many parts of America today, it no longer migrates. Gregarious, gathering in large herds of nearly 100 bison, mainly females (cows) and calves. Rolls and rubs in wallows to relieve insect bites. Uses its head and neck to push aside deep snow during winter to feed on the brown grass below.

The male (bull) is usually on its own or in a small group in fall and winter. A dominant bull will join a maternal herd late in summer before the rut. Cows at least 2-3 years old have reached maturity and are fertile for about 24 hours. A bull will curl its upper lip and extend its neck (flehmening) when around cows, perhaps to detect estrus. Bulls "tend" cows that are entering estrus rather than maintaining harems. Competing bulls strut near each other, showing off their large profile. Mature bulls sometimes face each other, charge, crash together headfirst and use their massive necks to push each other. Fights rarely result in an injury, but occasionally hooking or goring occurs.

sparring

Black Bear
Ursus americanus

Family: Bears (Ursidae)

Size: L 4½-6' (1.4-1.8 m); T 3-7" (7.5-18 cm); H 3-3½' (.9-1.1 m)

Weight: M 100-900 lb. (45-405 kg); F 90-525 lb. (41-236 kg)

Description: Nearly all black, sometimes brown, tan or cinnamon. Short round ears. Light brown snout. May have a small white patch on its chest. Short tail, which often goes unnoticed.

Origin/Age: native; 15-30 years

Compare: The only bear species in Arizona.

Habitat: all forest types, grasslands, elevations over 6,000' (1,830 m)

Home: den, underneath a fallen tree or in a rock crevice or cave, may dig a den 5-6' (1.5-1.8 m) deep with a small cavity at the end; male sometimes hibernates on the ground without shelter

Food: omnivore; leaves, nuts, roots, fruit, berries, grass, insects, fish, small mammals, carrion

Sounds: huffs, puffs or grunts and groans when walking, loud snorts made by air forced from nostrils, loud roars when fighting and occasionally when mating, motor-like humming when content

Breeding: Jun-Jul mating; 60-90 days gestation; implantation delayed until November after mating

Young: 1-5 (usually 2) cubs once every other year in January or February; born covered with fine dark fur, weighing only ½-1 lb. (.2-.5 kg)

347

claw marks

brown morph

scat

Signs: series of long narrow scars on tree trunks, usually as high as the bear can reach, made by scratching and biting, rub marks with snagged hair on the lower part of tree trunks or on large rocks, made by rubbing and scratching when shedding its winter coat; large dark cylindrical scat or piles of loose scat, usually contains berries and nuts, may contain animal hair, undigested plant stems and roots

Activity: diurnal, nocturnal; often seen feeding during the day

Tracks: hind paw 7-9" (18-23 cm) long, 5" (13 cm) wide with 5 toes, turns inward slightly, looks like a human track, forepaw 4" (10 cm) long, 5" (13 cm) wide with 5 toes, claw marks on all feet; fore and hind prints are parallel, hind paws fall several inches in front of fore prints; shuffles feet when walking

348

Stan's Notes: The Black Bear is unique to North America. Has a shuffling gait and frequently appears clumsy. It is not designed for speed, but can run up to 30 mph (48 km/h) for short distances. A powerful swimmer, however, and good at climbing trees. It has color vision, but poor eyesight and relies on smell to find most of its food. Often alone except for mating in early summer or when bears gather at a large food supply such as a garbage dump. Feeds heavily throughout summer, adding layers of fat for hibernation.

Hibernates up to five months per year starting in late fall. Heart rate drops from 70 to 10-20 beats per minute. Body temperature drops only 1-12°F (-17°C to -11°C), which is not enough to change mental functions. Doesn't eat, drink, pass feces or urinate during hibernation, yet can be roused and will move around in the den. The female can lose up to 40 percent of her body weight during hibernation.

cub

Male has a large territory of up to 15 square miles (39 sq. km) that often encompasses several female territories. Males fight each other for breeding rights and usually have scars from fights. The male bear matures at 3-4 years of age, but doesn't reach full size until 10-12 years. Males do not take part in raising young.

The female bear doesn't breed until it is 2-3 years of age. Females that have more body fat when entering hibernation will have more cubs than females with less fat. If a female does not have enough fat, she will not give birth. Mother bears, which average 177 pounds (80 kg), are approximately 250 times the size of newborns. A short gestation and tiny cubs are the result of the reproductive process during hibernation.

GLOSSARY

Browse: Twigs, buds and leaves that deer, elk and other animals eat.

Canid: A member of the Wolves, Foxes and Coyote family, which includes dogs.

Carnivore: An animal, such as a mink, fox or wolf, that eats the flesh of other animals for its main nutrition.

Carrion: Dead or decaying flesh. Carrion is a significant food source for many animal species.

Cecum: The large pouch that forms the beginning of the large intestine. Also known as the blind gut.

Cheek ruff: A gathering of long stiff hairs on each side of the face of an animal, ending in a downward point. Seen in bobcats.

Coprophagy: The act of reingesting fecal pellets. Coprophagy enables rabbits and hares to gain more nourishment since the pellets pass through the digestive system a second time.

Crepuscular: Active during the early morning and late evening hours as opposed to day or night. See *diurnal* and *nocturnal*.

Cud: Food regurgitated from the first stomach to the mouth, and chewed again. Cud is produced by hoofed animals such as deer or bison, which have a four-chambered stomach (ruminants).

Dewclaw: A nonfunctional (vestigial) digit on the feet of some animals, which does not touch the ground. Seen in deer and elk.

Direct register: The act of a hind paw landing or registering in the track left by a forepaw, resulting in two prints that appear like one track. Usually occurs when walking.

Diurnal: Active during daylight hours as opposed to nighttime hours. Opposite of *nocturnal*.

Drey: The nest of a squirrel.

Echolocation: A sensory system in bats, dolphins and some shrews, in which inaudible, high-pitched sounds are emitted and the returning echoes are interpreted to determine the direction and distance of objects such as prey.

Estrus: A state of sexual readiness in most female animals that immediately precedes ovulation, and the time when females are most receptive to mating. Also known as heat.

Extirpate: To hunt or trap into extinction in a region or state.

Flehmen: The lift of the upper lip and grimace an animal makes when it draws air into its mouth and over its Jacobson's organ, which is thought to help analyze the scents (pheromones) wafting in the air. Frequently seen in cats, deer and bison.

Gestation: Pregnancy. The period of development in the uterus of a mammal from conception up to birth.

Grizzled: Streaked or tipped with gray, or partly gray. Describes the appearance of some fur.

Guard hairs: The long outer hairs of an animal's coat, which provide warmth. Guard hairs are typically hollow and usually thicker and darker than the soft hairs underneath.

Haul out: A well-worn trail or area on the shore where an animal, such as an otter, climbs or hauls itself out of the water.

Herbivore: An animal, such as a rabbit, deer or elk, that eats plants for its main nutrition.

Hibernation: A torpid or lethargic state characterized by decreased heart rate, respiration and body temperature, and occurring in close quarters for long periods during winter. See *torpor*.

Hoary: Partly white or silver streaked, or tipped with white or silver. Describes the appearance of some fur.

Insectivore: An animal, such as a shrew, that eats insects as its main nutrition.

Keratin: A hard protein that is the chief component of the hair, nails, horns and hooves of an animal.

Microflora: Bacterial life living in the gut or first stomach of an animal. Microflora help break down food and aid in the digestive process.

Midden: A mound or deposit of pine cone parts and other refuse. A midden is evidence of a favorite feeding site of an animal such as a squirrel.

Morph: One of various distinct shapes, structural differences or colors of an animal. Color morphs do not change during the life of an animal.

Nictitating membrane: A second, inner eyelid, usually translucent, that protects and moistens the eye.

Nocturnal: Active during nighttime hours as opposed to daylight hours. Opposite of *diurnal*.

Nonretractile: That which cannot be drawn back or in. Describes the claws of a dog. Opposite of *retractile*.

Omnivore: An animal, such as a bear, that eats a wide range of foods including plants, insects and the flesh of other animals as its main nutrition.

Population: All individuals of a species within a specific area.

Predator: An animal that hunts, kills and eats other animals. See *prey*.

Prey: An animal that is hunted, killed and eaten by a predator. See *predator*.

Retractile: That which can be drawn back or in. Describes the claws of a cat. Opposite of *nonretractile*.

Rut: An annually recurring condition of sexual readiness and reproductive activity in mammals, such as deer and elk, that usually occurs in autumn. See *estrus*.

Scat: The fecal droppings of an animal.

Scent marking: A means of marking territory, signaling sexual availability or communicating an individual's identity. An animal scent marks with urine, feces or by secreting a tiny amount of odorous liquid from a gland, usually near the base of the tail, chin or feet, onto specific areas such as rocks, trees and stumps.

Semifossorial: Suited for burrowing or digging. Describes an animal such as a Kit Fox.

Semiprehensile: Suited for partially seizing, grasping or holding, especially by wrapping around an object, but not a means of full support. Describes the tail of an opossum.

Stride: In larger animals, the distance between individual tracks. In smaller animals such as weasels, the distance between sets of tracks.

Subnivean: Below the surface of snow, but above the surface of the earth. See *subterranean*.

Subterranean: Below the surface of the earth.

Talus: The accumulation of many rocks at the base of a cliff or mountain slope.

Torpor: A torpid or lethargic state resembling hibernation, characterized by decreased heart rate, respiration and body temperature, but usually shorter, lasting from a few hours to several days or weeks. See *hibernation*.

Tragus: A fleshy projection in the central part of the ear of most bats. The size and shape of the tragus may be used to help identify some bat species.

Tree rub: An area on small to medium trees where the bark has been scraped or stripped off. A tree rub is made by a male deer polishing his antlers in preparation for the rut.

Velvet: A soft, furry covering on antlers that contains many blood vessels, which support antler growth. Velvet is shed when antlers reach full size. Seen in the Deer family.

Vibrissae: Sensitive bristles and hairs, such as whiskers, that help an animal feel its way in the dark. Vibrissae are often on the face, legs and tail.

Wallow: A depression in the ground that is devoid of vegetation, where an animal, such as a bison, rolls around on its back to "bathe" in dirt.

HELPFUL RESOURCES

Emergency

For an animal bite, please seek medical attention at an emergency room or call 911. Injured or orphaned animals should be turned over to a licensed wildlife rehabilitator. Check your local listings for a rehabilitator near you.

Web Pages

The internet is a valuable place to learn more about mammals. You may find studying mammals on the net a fun way to discover additional information about them or to spend a long winter night. These web sites will assist you in your pursuit of mammals. If a web address doesn't work (they often change a bit), just enter the name of the group into a search engine to track down the new web address.

Site and Address:

Smithsonian Institution - North American Mammals
www.mnh2.si.edu/education/mna

The American Society of Mammalogists
www.mammalsociety.org

National Wildlife Rehabilitators Association
www.nwrawildlife.org/home.asp

International Wildlife Rehabilitation Council
www.iwrc-online.org

Arizona Game and Fish Department
www.azgfd.gov

Author Stan Tekiela's home page
www.naturesmart.com

Arizona's Artiodactyla Order

ORDER	SUBORDER	FAMILY	SUBFAMILY

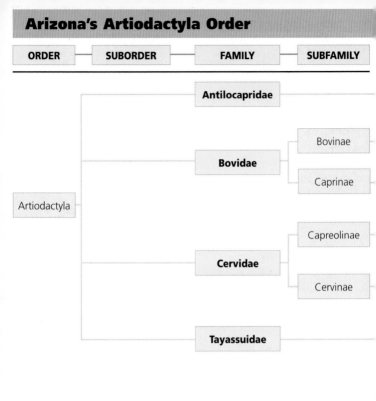

Artiodactyla

- Antilocapridae
- Bovidae
  - Bovinae
  - Caprinae
- Cervidae
  - Capreolinae
  - Cervinae
- Tayassuidae

Arizona's Perissodactyla Order

Perissodactyla — Equidae

Even-toed Hooved Animals

Pronghorn pg. 315
Antilocapra americana

American Bison pg. 343
Bison bison

Desert Bighorn Sheep pg. 339
Ovis canadensis nelsoni

White-tailed Deer pg. 319
Odocoileus virginianus couesi
Mule Deer pg. 323
Odocoileus hemionus

Elk pg. 327
Cervus elaphus

Javelina pg. 311
Pecari tajacu

Odd-toed Hooved Animals

Burro pg. 331
Equus asinus

Feral Horse pg. 335
Equus caballus

Box colors match the
corresponding section of the book.

Arizona's Carnivora Order

ORDER	SUBORDER	FAMILY	SUBFAMILY

Carnivora

- **Caniformia**
  - **Canidae**
  - **Mephitidae**
  - **Mustelidae**
    - Lutrinae
    - Mustelinae
    - Taxidiinae
  - **Procyonidae**
    - Procyoninae
  - **Ursidae**
    - Ursinae
- **Feliformia**
  - **Felidae**
    - Felinae
    - Pantherinae

Meat-eating Predators

Kit Fox pg. 271
Vulpes macrotis
Red Fox pg. 279
Vulpes vulpes

Gray Fox pg. 275
Urocyon cinereoargenteus

Coyote pg. 283
Canis latrans
Mexican Wolf pg. 287
Canis lupus baileyi

Western Spotted Skunk pg. 235
Spilogale gracilis

Hooded Skunk pg. 239
Mephitis macroura
Striped Skunk pg. 247
Mephitis mephitis

Hog-nosed Skunk pg. 243
Conepatus leuconotus

Northern River Otter pg. 231
Lontra canadensis

Long-tailed Weasel pg. 219
Mustela frenata
Black-footed Ferret pg. 223
Mustela nigripes

American Badger pg. 227
Taxidea taxus

Ringtail pg. 251
Bassariscus astutus

Northern Raccoon pg. 255
Procyon lotor

White-nosed Coati pg. 259
Nasua narica

Black Bear pg. 347
Ursus americanus

Ocelot pg. 291
Leopardus pardalis

Jaguarundi pg. 295
Herpailurus yagouaroundi

Bobcat pg. 299
Lynx rufus

Mountain Lion pg. 303
Puma concolor

Jaguar pg. 307
Panthera onca

Box colors match the
corresponding section of the book.

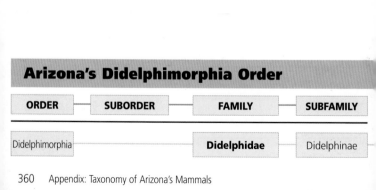

Arizona's Chiroptera Order

ORDER	SUBORDER	FAMILY	SUBFAMILY
Chiroptera		Phyllostomidae	Glossophaginae
			Phyllostominae
		Molossidae	Molossinae
	Microchiroptera	Vespertilionidae	Vespertilioninae

Arizona's Didelphimorphia Order

ORDER	SUBORDER	FAMILY	SUBFAMILY
Didelphimorphia		Didelphidae	Didelphinae

Bats

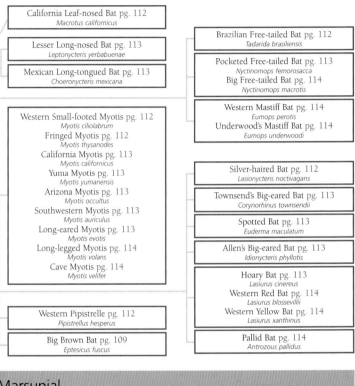

California Leaf-nosed Bat pg. 112
Macrotus californicus

Lesser Long-nosed Bat pg. 113
Leptonycteris yerbabuenae

Mexican Long-tongued Bat pg. 113
Choeronycteris mexicana

Western Small-footed Myotis pg. 112
Myotis ciliolabrum
Fringed Myotis pg. 112
Myotis thysanodes
California Myotis pg. 113
Myotis californicus
Yuma Myotis pg. 113
Myotis yumanensis
Arizona Myotis pg. 113
Myotis occultus
Southwestern Myotis pg. 113
Myotis auriculus
Long-eared Myotis pg. 113
Myotis evotis
Long-legged Myotis pg. 114
Myotis volans
Cave Myotis pg. 114
Myotis velifer

Western Pipistrelle pg. 112
Pipistrellus hesperus

Big Brown Bat pg. 109
Eptesicus fuscus

Brazilian Free-tailed Bat pg. 112
Tadarida brasiliensis

Pocketed Free-tailed Bat pg. 113
Nyctinomops femorosacca
Big Free-tailed Bat pg. 114
Nyctinomops macrotis

Western Mastiff Bat pg. 114
Eumops perotis
Underwood's Mastiff Bat pg. 114
Eumops underwoodi

Silver-haired Bat pg. 112
Lasionycteris noctivagans

Townsend's Big-eared Bat pg. 113
Corynorhinus townsendii

Spotted Bat pg. 113
Euderma maculatum

Allen's Big-eared Bat pg. 113
Idionycteris phyllotis

Hoary Bat pg. 113
Lasiurus cinereus
Western Red Bat pg. 114
Lasiurus blossevillii
Western Yellow Bat pg. 114
Lasiurus xanthinus

Pallid Bat pg. 114
Antrozous pallidus

Marsupial

Virginia Opossum pg. 267
Didelphis virginiana

Box colors match the
corresponding section of the book.

Arizona's Insectivora Order

ORDER	SUBORDER	FAMILY	SUBFAMILY

Insectivora		**Soricidae**	Soricinae

Arizona's Lagomorpha Order

ORDER	SUBORDER	FAMILY	SUBFAMILY

Lagomorpha		**Leporidae**	

Shrews

Desert Shrew pg. 39
Notiosorex crawfordi
Cockrum's Gray Shrew pg. 43
Notiosorex cockrumi

Dwarf Shrew pg. 43
Sorex nanus
Arizona Shrew pg. 43
Sorex arizonae
Merriam's Shrew pg. 43
Sorex merriami
Montane Shrew pg. 43
Sorex monticolus

Rabbits and Hares

Mountain Cottontail pg. 199
Sylvilagus nuttallii
Desert Cottontail pg. 203
Sylvilagus audubonii
Eastern Cottontail pg. 207
Sylvilagus floridanus

Black-tailed Jackrabbit pg. 211
Lepus californicus
Antelope Jackrabbit pg. 215
Lepus alleni

Box colors match the
corresponding section of the book.

Arizona's Rodentia Order

ORDER	SUBORDER	FAMILY	SUBFAMILY

	Hystricomorpha	**Erethizontidae**	
		Dipodidae	Zapodinae
			Arvicolinae
Rodentia	Myomorpha	**Muridae**	Murinae
			Sigmodontinae
	Sciuromorpha		

Continued on pages 366-367

Rodents

North American Porcupine pg. 263
Erethizon dorsatum

Western Jumping Mouse pg. 51
Zapus princeps

Southern Red-backed Vole pg. 95
Clethrionomys gapperi

Mexican Vole pg. 99
Microtus mexicanus
Montane Vole pg. 99
Microtus montanus
Long-tailed Vole pg. 99
Microtus longicaudus

Heather Vole pg. 99
Phenacomys intermedius

Muskrat pg. 101
Ondatra zibethicus

House Mouse pg. 64
Mus musculus

Black Rat pg. 93
Rattus rattus
Norway Rat pg. 91
Rattus norvegicus

Western Harvest Mouse pg. 55
Reithrodontomys megalotis
Plains Harvest Mouse pg. 59
Reithrodontomys montanus
Fulvous Harvest Mouse pg. 59
Reithrodontomys fulvescens

Southern Grasshopper Mouse pg. 67
Onychomys torridus
Mearn's Grasshopper Mouse pg. 71
Onychomys arenicola
Northern Grasshopper Mouse pg. 71
Onychomys leucogaster

Northern Pygmy Mouse pg. 64
Baiomys taylori

White-footed Mouse pg. 64
Peromyscus leucopus
Deer Mouse pg. 61
Peromyscus maniculatus
Mesquite Mouse pg. 65
Peromyscus merriami
Cactus Mouse pg. 64
Peromyscus eremicus
Pinyon Mouse pg. 65
Peromyscus truei
Canyon Mouse pg. 65
Peromyscus crinitus
Northern Rock Mouse pg. 65
Peromyscus nasutus
Brush Mouse pg. 65
Peromyscus boylii

Yellow-nosed Cotton Rat pg. 83
Sigmodon ochrognathus
Tawny-bellied Cotton Rat pg. 83
Sigmodon fulviventer
Arizona Cotton Rat pg. 79
Sigmodon arizonae
Hispid Cotton Rat pg. 83
Sigmodon hispidus

Arizona Woodrat pg. 89
Neotoma devia
Desert Woodrat pg. 89
Neotoma lepida
White-throated Woodrat pg. 85
Neotoma albigula
Stephen's Woodrat pg. 89
Neotoma stephensi
Bushy-tailed Woodrat pg. 89
Neotoma cinerea
Mexican Woodrat pg. 89
Neotoma mexicana

Box colors match the
corresponding section of the book.

Arizona's Rodentia Order

| ORDER | SUBORDER | FAMILY | SUBFAMILY |

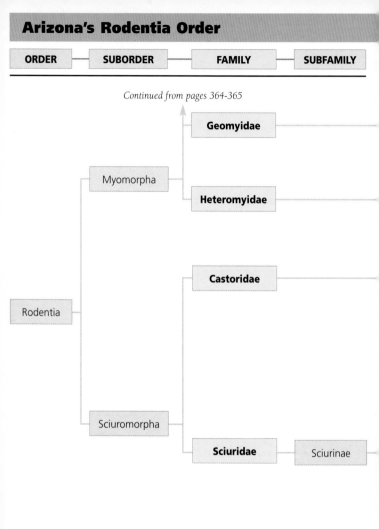

Continued from pages 364-365

Geomyidae

Myomorpha

Heteromyidae

Rodentia

Castoridae

Sciuromorpha

Sciuridae — Sciurinae

Rodents

Botta's Pocket Gopher pg. 193
Thomomys bottae
Southern Pocket Gopher pg. 197
Thomomys umbrinus
Northern Pocket Gopher pg. 197
Thomomys talpoides

Rock Pocket Mouse pg. 45
Chaetodipus intermedius
Desert Pocket Mouse pg. 48
Chaetodipus penicillatus
Long-tailed Pocket Mouse pg. 49
Chaetodipus formosus
Bailey's Pocket Mouse pg. 49
Chaetodipus baileyi
Hispid Pocket Mouse pg. 49
Chaetodipus hispidus

American Beaver pg. 105
Castor canadensis

Least Chipmunk pg. 117
Tamias minimus
Hopi Chipmunk pg. 121
Tamias rufus
Colorado Chipmunk pg. 125
Tamias quadrivittatus
Cliff Chipmunk pg. 129
Tamias dorsalis
Uinta Chipmunk pg. 133
Tamias umbrinus
Gray-collared Chipmunk pg. 137
Tamias cinereicollis

White-tailed Antelope Squirrel pg. 141
Ammospermophilus leucurus
Harris's Antelope Squirrel pg. 145
Ammospermophilus harrisii

Gunnison's Prairie Dog pg. 185
Cynomys gunnisoni
Black-tailed Prairie Dog pg. 189
Cynomys ludovicianus

Arizona Pocket Mouse pg. 48
Perognathus amplus
Little Pocket Mouse pg. 48
Perognathus longimembris
Apache Pocket Mouse pg. 48
Perognathus apache
Silky Pocket Mouse pg. 49
Perognathus flavus
Great Basin Pocket Mouse pg. 49
Perognathus parvus

Ord's Kangaroo Rat pg. 73
Dipodomys ordii
Merriam's Kangaroo Rat pg. 77
Dipodomys merriami
Chisel-toothed Kangaroo Rat pg. 77
Dipodomys microps
Desert Kangaroo Rat pg. 77
Dipodomys deserti
Banner-tailed Kangaroo Rat pg. 77
Dipodomys spectabilis

Spotted Ground Squirrel pg. 149
Spermophilus spilosoma
Round-tailed Ground Squirrel pg. 153
Spermophilus tereticaudus
Thirteen-lined Ground Squirrel pg. 157
Spermophilus tridecemlineatus
Golden-mantled Ground Squirrel pg. 161
Spermophilus lateralis
Rock Squirrel pg. 165
Spermophilus variegatus

Red Squirrel pg. 169
Tamiasciurus hudsonicus

Abert's Squirrel pg. 173
Sciurus aberti
Arizona Gray Squirrel pg. 177
Sciurus arizonensis
Mexican Fox Squirrel pg. 181
Sciurus nayaritensis

Box colors match the
corresponding section of the book.

CHECK LIST/INDEX BY SPECIES

Use the boxes to check the mammals you've seen.

PHOTO CREDITS

Dr. J. Scott Altenbach: 113 (Pocketed, Lesser), 114 (Western Mastiff, Underwood's)

Aaron M. Ambos: 77 (Chisel-toothed)

Randall D. Babb: 114 (Yellow), 268 (main)

Robert Baker: 43 (Arizona)

Roger W. Barbour: 52

David J. Behmer: 120, 122 (inset)

Troy L. Best/American Society of Mammalogists: 77 (Desert), 122 (main)

Rick and Nora Bowers: 46, 49 (Bailey's, Hispid), 54, 62, 64 (Cactus), 65 (Northern), 74 (inset), 77 (Merriam's), 83 (Yellow-nosed, Hispid), 84, 86, 89 (Stephen's), 99 (Mexican), 112 (Leaf-nosed, Pipistrelle, Brazilian), 113 (California, Townsend's, Arizona, Southwestern, Mexican), 114 (Long-legged, Red, Cave, Free-tailed), 130 (all), 132, 134 (main, top and bottom insets), 136, 138, 142 (top inset), 154 (main), 172, 180, 182 (both), 184, 186 (all), 192, 194 (both), 197 (Northern), 214, 216 (top inset), 222, 224 (main), 236, 246, 248 (main), 260 (both insets), 270, 272 (all), 288 (main, left inset), 292, 293, 294, 296, 306, 312 (middle and right insets), 332 (both)

Karen J. Carter: 48 (Little)

Kathy Adams Clark/KAC Productions: 150

E. R. Degginger/Dembinsky Photo Associates: 89 (Arizona)

Phil A. Dotson/Photo Researchers, Inc.: 89 (Bushy-tailed), 252 (main)

Kevin Doxstater: 174 (right inset)

Jerry Dragoo: 240 (main), 242, 244 (main)

R. B. Forbes/American Society of Mammalogists: 89 (Mexican)

Larry Jon Friesen: 93

Tony Gallucci: 244 (bottom inset)

Christine Hass: 240 (inset), 268 (bottom left inset)

John O. Hollister: 238

Gerald C. Kelley/Photo Researchers, Inc.: 252 (inset)

Gary Kramer: 140, 142 (bottom inset)

Stephen J. Krasemann/Photo Researchers, Inc.: 234

Dwight Kuhn: 71 (Northern)

Maslowski Productions: 218, 221

Emil McCain, Borderlands Jaguar Detection Project: 308

Joe McDonald: 197 (Southern)

Tom McHugh/Photo Researchers, Inc.: 50, 89 (Desert)

Gary Meszaros/Dembinsky Photo Associates: 128

C. Allan Morgan: 48 (Arizona)

National Park Service: 244 (top inset)

Stan Osolinski/Dembinsky Photo Associates: 220

B. Moose Peterson/Wildlife Research Photography: 49 (Great), 99 (Long-tailed), 113 (Long-eared), 134 (middle inset), 142 (main)

Jim Roetzel/Dembinsky Photo Associates: 250

Cecil Schwalbe: 40

Stan Tekiela: 44, 48 (Desert), 49 (Silky), 59 (Fulvous), 60, 64 (Pygmy, House, White-footed), 65 (Brush), 66, 68, 72, 74 (main), 78, 80, 83 (Tawny-bellied), 87, 90, 92 (both), 94, 96, 100, 102 (all), 104, 106 (all), 108, 110 (inset), 112 (Silver-haired), 113 (Hoary), 114 (Pallid), 116, 118 (both), 124, 126 (all), 144, 146 (both), 152, 154 (both insets), 156, 158 (all), 160, 162 (all), 164, 166 (all), 168, 170 (all), 174 (main, left inset), 176, 178 (both), 188, 190 (all), 198, 200 (all), 202, 204 (both), 206, 208 (all), 209, 210, 212 (both), 216 (main, bottom inset), 224 (inset), 226, 228 (all), 230, 232 (all), 248 (both insets), 254, 256 (both), 257, 258, 260 (main), 262, 264 (all), 265, 266, 268 (main, top and right insets), 274, 276 (all), 277 (both), 278, 280 (all), 281 (both), 282, 284 (all), 285, 286, 288 (right inset), 290, 298, 300 (all), 301, 302, 304 (all), 305, 310, 312 (main, top and bottom left insets), 314, 316 (all), 318, 320 (all), 321, 322, 324 (all), 326, 328 (all), 330, 334, 336 (all), 338, 340 (all), 342, 344 (all), 346, 348 (all), 349

Merlin D. Tuttle/Bat Conservation International, Inc.: 110 (main), 112 (Small-footed), 113 (Spotted, Yuma, Allen's)

John and Gloria Tveten: 56, 112 (Fringed)

John and Gloria Tveten/KAC Productions: 38, 43 (Dwarf), 48 (Apache), 59 (Plains), 65 (Pinyon), 71 (Mearn's), 77 (Banner-tailed), 99 (Montane), 148

www.birdandhike.com: 49 (Long-tailed)

To the best of the publisher's knowledge, all photos but one were of live mammals. Some were photographed in a controlled condition.

ABOUT THE AUTHOR

Stan Tekiela is a naturalist, author and wildlife photographer with a Bachelor of Science degree in Natural History from the University of Minnesota. He has been a professional naturalist for more than 20 years and is a member of the Minnesota Naturalists' Association, Outdoor Writers Association of America, North American Nature Photography Association and Canon Professional Services. Stan actively studies and photographs wildlife throughout the United States. He has received various national and regional awards for outdoor education and writing. His syndicated nature column appears in over 20 cities and his wildlife programs are broadcast on a number of Midwest radio stations. For about two decades, Stan has authored more than 100 field guides, nature appreciation books and wildlife audio CDs for nearly every state in the nation, presenting many species of birds, mammals, reptiles and amphibians, trees, wildflowers and cacti. His Arizona field guides include *Birds of Arizona*, *Mammals of Arizona*, *Trees of Arizona*, *Wildflowers of Arizona* and *Cactus of Arizona*.

Stan resides in Victoria, Minnesota, with his wife, Katherine, and daughter, Abigail. He can be contacted via his web page at www.naturesmart.com.